[ED. F. KRUSE OF BLUE BELL CREAMERIES]

"The American Dream means giving it your all, trying your hardest, accomplishing something. And then I'd add to that, giving something back. No definition of a successful life can do anything but include serving others."

—President George H. W. Bush, in a June 2, 1995 interview

Ed. F. Kruse *of* Blue Bell Creameries

Dorothy McLeod MacInerney

FOREWORD BY RYAN CROCKER

Texas A&M University Press
COLLEGE STATION

∞ This paper meets the requirements of ANSI/NISO z39.48-1992
(Permanence of Paper).
Binding materials have been chosen for durability.

LIBRARY OF CONGRESS CATALOGING-IN-PUBLICATION DATA

MacInerney, Dorothy McLeod, author.
Ed F. Kruse of Blue Bell Creameries / Dorothy McLeod MacInerney. —
First edition.
pages cm
Includes bibliographical references and index.
ISBN 978-1-62349-363-9 (cloth: alk. paper) —
ISBN 978-1-62349-364-6 (ebook)
ISBN 979-1-64843-323-8 (paperback)
1. Kruse, Ed F., 1928–2015 2. Businessmen—Texas—Brenham—Biography.
3. Blue Bell Creameries—History. 4. Ice cream industry—Texas—
Brenham—History. I. Title.
HD9281.U52K786 2016
338.7′6374092—dc23
[B]
2015018647

[Contents]

[Foreword]

FEW PEOPLE have had more impact on this part of Texas than the Kruse family of Brenham. Led by Edward and Howard, the Kruses have shown for decades that success in business and success in life are mutually reinforcing concepts.

Dorothy MacInerney has written a delightful biography of Ed Kruse that is really the story of an approach to living that affects and touches us all (she is also the author of *Blue Bell Ice Cream: A Century at the Little Creamery in Brenham, Texas 1907–2007*). Everyone who knew Ed knows some of his "Edisms," captured here in their entirety (well, there will always be a few more). Taken together, the 34 Edisms are as comprehensive and universal a philosophy as you are likely to see. Individually and collectively, they capture the essence of Ed Kruse and an extraordinary way of life.

I have been privileged, as have so many others, to benefit from his conviction expressed in Edism #9 (It's good to be benevolent) and #24 (If you can do some good, do it now). The Bush School of Government and Public Service at Texas A&M University, where I am the dean, has grown into one of the best schools of public service in the nation with the help of very generous support from the Kruses. Our mission is to prepare young men and women to fulfill the 41st President's vision of public service as a noble calling. That sounds a lot like an Edism, and it is no surprise that Ed Kruse and George H. W. Bush were close friends.

Dr. MacInerney grabs your attention in the first pages with an account of a near-fatal plane crash that Ed described to his family with characteristic understatement as "a problem with the landing gear" (Edism #34: It's good to be humble). She weaves the story of Ed's early years and young adulthood with that of Blue Bell's own coming of age, with particular focus on Ed's time at A&M. Ed embodied the Aggie core values of excellence, integrity, leadership, loyalty, respect, and selfless service—these are what underlie the Edisms. Together with family and the world's best ice cream, A&M was a central element in Ed's life. It wasn't always easy. As Dr. MacInerney notes, if you could get through your freshman year in the 1940s, you could get through almost anything. Ed credited A&M with shaping his life, and he repaid that contribution many times over.

The story of Ed Kruse and the story of Blue Bell are inseparable. Ed was only 23 when he took over as manager following the early death of his father. In that year (1951), there were just 35 employees and $250,000 in annual sales. Ed also faced significant debt, but he had the company in the black his first full year in charge. Howard joined him in 1954 after his graduation from A&M and service in the Army, and under their leadership, Blue Bell's trajectory was almost unimaginable.

Ed had a lot of company on his journey, no one more important than his wonderful wife Evelyn who was by his side for 65 years. Dr. MacInerney relates the warming story of their courtship. If not love at first sight, it was pretty close. After their third date, Ed announced with his signature emphasis, "I'm going to marry that girl! *Period.*" They started with a great deal of love but not much money. Their search for an affordable apartment in Fort Worth was that of hopeful newlyweds everywhere.

It was not always an easy road. Ed and Evelyn faced adversity and tragedy that would have broken lesser people. They emerged stronger and even more committed to each other (Edism #8: Each of us was put on Earth for some good reason). Adversity has recently struck Blue Bell. Under CEO and president Paul Kruse, Ed's son, the company will weather this storm, guided by Edisms—do not compromise your principles, do what you say you're going to do, stand up for what's right, and, perhaps most important: No one ever gets lost on a straight road.

As I write this, it is spring in the Brazos Valley. The Aggies are playing at home, and it's time to head over to Olsen Field at Blue Bell Park, an absolute gem after a $7 million renovation by Ed and Howard. The team calls it the "sweetest facility in college baseball." It is just one of the many gifts from these extraordinary philanthropists and great Americans.

Play ball. *Period.*

RYAN CROCKER
Dean and Holder of the Edward and Howard Kruse Endowed Chair
Bush School of Government and Public Service
Texas A&M University

[Acknowledgments]

DOROTHY MCLEOD MACINERNEY is probably the most unlikely person to be listed as the author of this book. Yes, she wrote the words down and composed them, but the people who contributed significant information and lively accounts are the ones to be recognized and celebrated.

Foremost is Ed. F. Kruse. This is his story from beginning to end. He came to every interview with his list of sayings that have been so important to him throughout his life. He always had a lineup of people he wanted to discuss. Occasionally, he brought a speech, letter, photo, joke, or treasured document to share. The last subject he wanted to address was himself. Over the months, however, the varied pieces from all parts of his life fell into place, and his story emerged. The format of this book should have been a memoir or an autobiography, but Ed Kruse never would have written in the first person. You will understand why as the narrative progresses.

Aiding the entire fact-finding process was Ruth Goeke, Ed Kruse's invaluable executive administrator for almost 50 years. She displayed intense interest in this project and guided it along in more ways than can ever be properly acknowledged. Ruth could have written this book blindfolded with her hands tied behind her back. Instead, she constantly provided information that Ed probably didn't realize he still had in his files. For example, there were handwritten notes for speeches he delivered. One scrap of paper was a bet between Ed and his brother Howard on the future of the ice cream industry. Another was a set of questions Ed developed to ask contestants in a beauty contest he was preparing to judge. Ruth tracked down a genealogical study of the Kruse family to provide background; plowed through ancient board of directors' minutes to answer arcane questions; and steadily supplied newspaper and magazine articles, actual speeches, letters, statistics, and so much more. Ruth read and edited the manuscript several times and clearly lamented when parts had to be cut. Ed Kruse did not want the book to be any longer than what he was willing to sit down to read! Ruth will need to do the sequel and tell the rest of the story.

Karen Kruse Hall, Ed's daughter, also contributed greatly to the narrative. She willingly and accurately fleshed out stories that her father mentioned during interviews. She strongly supported the project and came to each interview with a twinkle in her eye, a smile on her lips, and an eagerness to share Kruse family lore. Karen also enhanced the manuscript through various readings and suggestions. Her husband, Wes Hall, even proposed the "hook" for the book.

Two other people, Evelyn Tiaden Kruse and Paul W. Kruse, were certainly capable of telling Ed's story as well. Evelyn met Ed as a teenager and married him a year after he graduated from Texas A&M. She knew him better than anyone in the world and offered a meaningful personal perspective to the book. Paul Kruse, Ed's surviving son and now CEO, president, and chairman of the board of Blue Bell Creameries, worked with Ed Kruse almost daily for thirty years. Paul understands completely—and emulates faithfully—his father's business philosophy. Paul has clear recollections of business transactions, family legends, and other matters presented in this account.

Ed Kruse, Ruth Goeke, Karen Kruse Hall, Evelyn Kruse, or Paul Kruse could have been—and maybe should have been—the author of the book you're holding in your hand. Sincerest thanks go to each of them for giving me the honor and privilege to learn more about Blue Bell Creameries and the Kruse family. I am also grateful for their support, time, and encouragement in the process of writing down this inspiring and worthwhile story.

Special gratitude is reserved for Ryan C. Crocker, dean of the Bush School of Government and Public Service at Texas A&M University, for his foreword to this book. Dean Crocker not only put considerable time, effort, and thought into his richly written words, but he's also a fervent Kruse and Blue Bell supporter. Thank you, too, Dean Crocker, for your honorable, significant, and longstanding service to our country.

Several other people need to be mentioned and thanked. Patricia I. Ryan begged Ed Kruse for years to write his memoir. Kathleen Rice helped pare down the manuscript and provided sustained backing during our daily 6:30 a.m. conversations. Captain Midnight—also known as William Warren Rogers, professor emeritus at Florida State University—has been a valuable mentor. Many people at Blue Bell Creameries contributed information and photos. They include, but are not limited to, Joe Robertson, Jenny Van Dorf, Kelli Remmert, and Kim Hoff. Without *all* the amazing folks at Blue Bell Creameries over the past 108 years, there would be no story to tell.

The experts at Texas A&M University Press have provided their talents, handholding, patience, and good cheer. Heartfelt thanks go to Charles Backus, Thom Lemmons, Katie Duelm, Kari Lucke, Holli Koster, Gayla Christiansen, Sue Gaines, and so many others who worked behind the scenes. I send a special nod of gratitude to one of the anonymous reviewers of the manuscript at Texas A&M University Press. That perceptive person rewarded the entire project when stating, "A real lesson learned will be that good guys who operate honestly and fairly, with their employees and their customers, can win!" Thank you for grasping the gist of the message.

For buoying up, I always turn to the Galveston Girls, the Workout Sisters, the Art History Book Club, the No Pressure Book Club, and many other friends. My heart, soul, and glee revolve around Buddy, Ed, Doug, Eric, Kim, Karen, Dylan, Gillian, Erin, Connor, Cullen, Abby, Ian, and our extended family.

My deepest thanks to all of you.

Note to Readers

With the exception of the foreword and the afterword, this book entered the publication process at Texas A&M University Press before the recall of all Blue Bell products in the spring of 2015. Because the primary focus here is Ed. F. Kruse's life, the voluntary product recall lies outside the scope of this book.

Chapter One

Each of us was put on Earth

for some good reason.

• EDISM #8 •

THE FUEL GAUGE READ EMPTY. Nevertheless, Tom insisted that his Piper PA-31P continue its flight to Presidio, Texas, with its cargo of six men and hundreds of pounds of frozen fish. Sitting in the copilot's seat, Ed. F. Kruse breathed a sigh of relief when he spotted the town below. Expecting Tom to fly a few miles north to the designated airfield, Ed was surprised when Tom began circling a tiny crop-duster landing strip. He soon understood why.

As Tom began to descend, one of the engines cut out. As he was positioning to land, the other engine stopped. Mercifully, both sputtered to life again. But a gusty tailwind was forcing the plane toward the short, dirt runway much too fast.

Going between 80 and 90 mph, the plane hit the landing strip midway down its length and quickly came to the end—a dirt embankment topped by a barbed-wire fence.

Tom shot the plane over the barrier, which stripped the landing gear. The plane tumbled, pancaked, then landed upside down.

The next thing Ed knew was that he was suspended in time and space. He also smelled smoke. He remembered hearing the rocks and bushes scraping against the fuselage and thinking that if he survived the crash, he would be a vegetable. Disoriented, he finally discovered he could move his arms. Checking to be sure the rest of his body was intact, he realized he was, in fact, upside down but still strapped into his seat. Worried about the burning left wing, Ed focused on escape.

He struggled to unbuckle the seat belt and then crawled through a window that his friend and fellow passenger Doc Giddings had kicked out. Four of the six men were now outside the plane—injured but upright. Tom was still scrunched into the pilot's seat, and the sixth passenger was aware enough to know that his back was broken.

Fortunately, the fire on the left wing had burned itself out—for lack of fuel. Ed helped dislodge Tom from the pilot's seat, and, with concerted effort, the group was able to remove the other man from the plane without further harming his spine. Emergency help from Presidio arrived and prepared to transport Ed's friend with the broken back to El Paso. The others waited an hour and a half for an ambulance from Alpine to reach the scene and take them to the hospital there.

The medical personnel treated Ed's scrapes, gashes, and scratches and wanted to admit him for observation, suspecting he had suffered a concussion. Ed thought that unnecessary and waited for someone from his hometown, Brenham, Texas, to drive the 500 miles out west to pick him up. He called his wife, Evelyn, to let her know that he would be late—"a problem with the landing gear," he said. When he later related the story to others, he joked about how lucky they had been that the plane didn't continue to burn: "If there had been more fuel in the plane, we wouldn't have crash-landed in the first place! *Period.*"

Despite efforts to make light of this incident and brush things off, it was at this point in his life that Ed. F. Kruse figured that God had put him—and kept him—on Earth for some good reason. In fact, had Ed died in the accident, a potential obituary would have revealed the extremely successful life he had already lived to that point:

> Edward Fred Kruse, age 55, died in an airplane crash in Presidio, Texas, at 12:40 p.m. on Wednesday, February 15, 1984. His death came at the end of an enjoyable bass fishing trip with close friends in Los Mochis, Mexico.
>
> Born on March 15, 1928, Ed. F. Kruse was the first son and third child of E. F. and Bertha (Quebe) Kruse of Brenham, Texas. His father managed Blue Bell Creameries, Inc. from 1919 until his unanticipated death in 1951. The board of directors then offered the position of manager to Ed, a 23-year-old route supervisor at Blue Bell. Ed had worked for Blue Bell since the age of 13, had achieved a BS degree in dairy manufacturing from Texas A&M University in 1949, and had spent 18 months at the ice cream division of Swift and Company before returning to Blue Bell full-time.
>
> As manager, then president and CEO, of Blue Bell

Creameries for 33 years, Ed guided the company from a tiny creamery competing with twenty-five others in Central Texas to one taking on the national brands—Carnation, Borden, Swift, Superior, and Foremost—in Houston, Austin, Dallas, Fort Worth, and parts of Louisiana and Oklahoma.

Ed was well known in the dairy industry and served in several prominent positions in its trade organizations. He was secretary and, in 1973, president of the Dairy Products Institute of Texas. He held a three-year term as president of the Dixie Dairy Products Association from 1978 to 1982. He supported the International Association of Ice Cream Manufacturers, located in Washington, DC, by joining the board of directors in 1971, being elected vice-chairman in 1982, and serving as the chairman from 1983 until his death—the first Texan to attain that position.

Ed. F. Kruse. Courtesy of Ed. F. and Evelyn Kruse

Ed was also active in local community affairs, serving as president of the Brenham Rotary Club from 1958 to 1959, president of the Brenham Industrial Foundation in 1966, and chairman of the board of both First National Bank and Mbank. He taught Sunday school, led Boy Scout troops, and held various positions at St. Paul's Evangelical Lutheran Church, including president of the congregation.

He married Evelyn Delores Tiaden on June 18, 1950. They were the proud parents of four children who followed in Ed's footsteps and graduated from Texas A&M University—Karen ('73), Ken ('75), Paul ('77), and Neil ('80).

Thankfully, there was no need for such an obituary. The extensive biographical information demonstrates, however, that by 1984 Ed. F. Kruse had made many positive contributions to society. Had he died a mere month before his fifty-sixth birthday, he would have left an indelible impression

Ed Kruse and his five fishing companions survived this Piper PA-31P plane crash on February 15, 1984.
Courtesy of Ed. F. and Evelyn Kruse

on the community, the state, and the ice cream industry, just as his father had done when he passed away at age 56. Ed Kruse strongly believed that God felt there was much more for him to accomplish.

And he did just that: Ed continued to take the leading role at Blue Bell Creameries until 1993, when he cut his workweek in half and handed over the title of CEO to his brother Howard. At that point, Ed retained his position as chairman of the board and expert consultant. By the time Howard retired in 2004, the brothers had witnessed their company's expansion into twelve states—quite an achievement for the "little creamery in Brenham." Blue Bell had become the third best-selling ice cream brand in the United States, behind Dreyer's/Edy's and Breyers. Ed's son Paul W. Kruse has since guided the company's additional successes.

Tragically, Ed lost two of his sons, both when they were 45 years old. Ken drowned in 1999, and Neil succumbed to inoperable cancer in 2003. Not understanding why these devastating heartbreaks happened to him and Evelyn, Ed refused to shake his fist at God. Instead, he focused on the positive and strove to do the next right thing. Ironically, Ed himself battled cancer—and won.

Ed guided Blue Bell Creameries until the age of 85. On February 20, 2014, he resigned as chairman of the board. For the first time since he was

13 years old, he had no formal responsibilities in the company, except as a member of the board of directors. Nevertheless, he was a busy, productive man.

For example, he continued to dote on Evelyn—they celebrated their sixty-fifth wedding anniversary on June 18, 2015. He followed daughter Karen's and son Paul's busy lives with pride. Somehow, he kept up with his twenty-two grandchildren and three great-grandchildren. He went to his office at Blue Bell several times a week, looked through the "second-class mail that finds its way to my desk," and talked to folks about what's going on in the company. He spent much time and energy deciding how to give back to his community. He planned trips for the entire family to enjoy. He attended Brenham High School Cubs' sporting events and paid close attention to the school's honor rolls posted in the *Brenham Banner-Press*—always on the lookout for future leaders at Blue Bell and in Brenham. He supported his beloved Texas A&M University in countless ways, along with many other institutions. He lunched with a group of friends biweekly to discuss and solve local, state, national, and international problems.

Ed was always a bundle of energy. He readily admitted that he would have been diagnosed with ADHD if born at a later time. And he constantly added items to his bucket list.

One of the most intriguing challenges on that agenda was to chronicle his life's story. Ed was a modest man. In no way did he attribute the success of Blue Bell Creameries to himself. He liked to think that he, at least, had a hand in hiring some of the amazingly talented and dedicated people who make and sell the best ice cream in the country. And, perhaps, a few of the decisions he made encouraged everyone in the company to head in the same direction at the same time—providing a strong atmosphere for teamwork. But according to Ed, the folks at Blue Bell definitely deserved the praise for the achievements of the little creamery in Brenham.

Likewise, he gave the credit to Evelyn for their outstanding children. He was busy at work during those formative years. Although he did come home for dinner each night and participated in every way he could, Evelyn was on duty 24/7/365.

Ed was reserved about the many contributions he made to his community, saying that in different situations he only used an idea he had come across before . . . was simply one of many who made donations to the cause . . . happened to see the need before others did . . . gave back because it was the natural thing to do, and so on.

Nevertheless, as Ed surveyed a successful and rewarding life, he wondered if he had something to share with others. What immediately came to mind were several guiding principles that helped him throughout his life. These suggestions derived from his father, common sense, Benjamin Franklin, the Bible, and other age-old sources. The vast majority he picked up during tough or uncomfortable experiences.

A prime example occurred when Ed was a student at Texas A&M University. A member of the swim team, Ed traveled to meets in various parts of Texas, Oklahoma, Arkansas, and Kansas. The national water-polo championships took the Aggie swimmers as far away as Detroit, Michigan. To remember each trip, Ed pilfered a monogrammed towel from the hotel in which the team stayed. He rationalized that Texas A&M had more than paid for the towels because of the high hotel rates.

One weekend while Ed was home in Brenham, his mother discovered Ed's hidden treasure. She told his father, E. F., and the ensuing conversation went something like this:

E. F.: "Son, where'd you get these towels?"
Ed: "From the various hotels where we stayed for swim meets."
E. F.: "I see. Did they give them to you?"
Ed: "No, sir."
E. F.: "Did you ask the hotel if it was okay to take them?"
Ed: "No, sir."
E. F.: "So you just took them?"
Ed: "Yes, sir."
E. F.: "You know that's wrong, don't you?"
Ed: "Yes, sir."
E. F.: "I want you to mail each towel back to the proper hotel with a letter of apology. Son, no one ever gets lost on a straight road."

Ed did as instructed and realized that his father was right. He felt fortunate to have learned such a valuable lesson as a young man and to be able to apply it to other personal and business situations throughout his life.

Included here are thirty-two additional "Edisms," arranged in no order of importance or chronology. Most of them will be familiar—even Ed admitted in Edism #6 that he never had an original thought but sometimes combined ideas in an effective way for the situation at hand. Admittedly, many other sayings are in wide circulation and certainly have equal value. In providing this particular list, Ed simply recognized and emphasized that these specific adages served him well.

#1   No one ever gets lost on a straight road.

#2   It's important to do what's right and ethical, not merely what's legal.

#3   Integrity is not negotiable.

#4   There's no telling how much good you can do if you don't mind who gets the credit.

#5   You can whip almost any problem if you work hard enough and long enough.

#6   Few people have original thoughts, so it's wise to take ideas from others and put them together.

#7   Aptitude is important, but so is attitude.

#8   Each of us was put on Earth for some good reason.

#9   It's good to be benevolent.

#10   Moderation is the key.

#11   It's a cinch by the inch, hard by the yard.

#12   It's more blessed to give than to receive.

#13   Admit your mistakes—with its corollary: Forget excuses.

#14   Keep things in perspective.

#15   Maintain a sense of humor.

#16   Don't assume. (It makes an "ass" out of "u" and "me.")

#17   Learn to communicate effectively.

#18   Work hard—the harder you work, the luckier you get.

#19   Hire honor students for administrative positions.

#20   Do not compromise your principles.

#21   Thank people who have helped you.

#22   Be honest in all your dealings.

#23   Never do anything that your conscience tells you is wrong.

#24   If you can do some good, do it now.

#25   Be prepared.

#26   Do what you say you're going to do.

#27   Stand up for what's right.

#28   Be strong enough to delay gratification.

#29   Follow the Golden Rule. (Do unto others as you would have them do unto you.)

#30   Work, don't worry.

#31   Do a common job uncommonly well.

#32   Think ahead.

#33   Set goals and work toward them.

Some readers can stop right here. They can apply Edisms to their lives, and the suggestions may make a positive impact. Ed believed that simply keeping the Edisms handy, reviewing them occasionally, and applying them whenever appropriate could enhance the quality of one's life. In fact, he carried the list with him and referred to it often—even adding a new entry on occasion. (He said as long as he's breathing, he's learning.)

However, experiencing the lessons in context makes for an interesting journey. You may even encounter more than you expected. The hope is that you will continue to read this account about how Ed Kruse grew up, took his turn as manager of Blue Bell Creameries, helped Evelyn raise their children, retired, and gave back to the community.

If you choose this route, there is a caveat: this is the story of Ed Kruse. Nevertheless, in the sections where Blue Bell is discussed, it is difficult to extricate him solely from the synergy that is Blue Bell Creameries itself. Blue Bell is a strong team, made up of excellent players. Ed had the privilege to play most of the positions and to coach the team for many years.

As Ed often said, "People are the most important asset we have at Blue Bell. *Period.*" Ed was one of those talented individuals. He and other team members have a similar story to tell, but their paths necessarily merge from different directions and perspectives.

Please accompany me as we travel through time with Ed and watch his tried-and-true principles shape a life productively, meaningfully, and gratefully lived.

Chapter Two

> # Work hard—the harder you work, the luckier you get.
>
> • EDISM #18 •

EDWARD FRED KRUSE was born on March 15, 1928, in Brenham, Texas. He was named for his father Eddie Fritz Kruse but was not a "junior" because of the Anglicisation of his father's German name. Throughout their lives, the two distinguished themselves as E. F. Kruse (father) and Ed. F. Kruse (son).

Ordinarily, one would not associate one's young years with "working hard," but Ed Kruse was born into a family where industriousness was constantly practiced and valued.

E. F. Kruse managed Blue Bell Creameries from 7:30 a.m. to 6:00 p.m. six days a week. He was also at the office two hours on Sundays before church to receive fresh cream from the local farmers. Whereas Blue Bell Creameries produces only ice cream today, it began as the Brenham Creamery Company in 1907 and made only butter, with ice cream being first produced in 1911.

The company struggled mightily in its early years. The original investors were not butter makers but local merchants who came up with a winning strategy for the entire community. The Brenham Creamery Company bought extra cream from nearby farmers whose main crops were corn and cotton. With a small, steady income, the farmers could then afford to purchase staples and dry goods from the Brenham merchants throughout the year, not just when their crops were harvested and sold in the fall. Meanwhile, the Brenham Creamery Company used the cream from the farmers' cows to produce a constant supply of butter for the townsfolk. Everyone benefited from the plan.

The difficulty arose in the hands-on management of the creamery. The investors, who focused on their own businesses, hired and fired several

Blue Bell Creameries began as the Brenham Creamery Company in 1907. E. F. Kruse renamed the business in 1930 to reflect his love of the purple wildflowers that bloom profusely in Central Texas in August, the height of ice cream season. *Courtesy of Blue Bell Creameries*

managers of varying abilities. Even after the company added ice cream to its product line, the business nearly failed. As a last resort, H. F. Hohlt, president of the board of directors, advanced additional funds to the creamery and hired as manager a well-respected and intelligent area teacher who was winding up his service to his country in World War I.

When 23-year-old E. F. Kruse first joined the company in 1919, he labored long and hard to get the floundering and neglected creamery into the black—not cashing his own paychecks for six months until finances were on better footing. He saw his valiant efforts pay off; luck had nothing to do with it.

E. F.'s few "leisure" hours were filled with church, American Legion, and other community responsibilities. He also took an active role in the state dairy industry. Indeed, he was a busy man.

Bertha Quebe Kruse, Ed's mother, managed her growing family and bustling home. Ed was the middle child of five. Bertha was born in 1921, Mildred in 1923, Ed in 1928, Howard in 1930, and Evelyn Ann in 1934. Another older sister, Edwina (born in 1927), died of whooping cough at the age of four weeks.

The family's house on West Fourth Street (now College Avenue) was given to Ed's parents as a wedding present from Bertha's father, Henry Quebe. It was a two-story, white wooden structure built in the 1880s. Gingerbread trim adorned the tops of the porches and eaves of the roof, which was flat and made of copper. E. F. and Bertha split the home into four apartments. Their family lived in one apartment downstairs and rented the other three out. Bertha was responsible for that portion of the income stream.

Bertha also contributed to the family coffers by sewing for her family and making handicrafts to decorate their home. She participated in the American Legion Auxiliary and in various activities at the family's church, St. Paul's Evangelical Lutheran Church. The Kruses actually lived next door to St. Paul's, so they felt obligated to maintain their property in pristine condition. From an early age, the Kruse children helped their mother in her rose garden. Ed and Howard raked the sycamore and magnolia leaves in the fall as small boys and graduated to cutting the grass during the summers, edging the sidewalk with a hoe.

Another of young Ed's chores was chopping wood in the backyard, gathering kindling, and hauling it all into the house to fuel the pot-bellied stove. Ed claimed that he thought his name was "Git Wood" until he was 10 years old.

Ed helped make sausage from the hogs the Kruses purchased each winter from Ed's uncles, who farmed in the areas surrounding Brenham. He raised chickens in the backyard, even though they lived in town.

Ed and his younger brother Howard woke up at 6 a.m. on Monday mornings in the summertime to assist their parents with the laundry. Outside, water from the cistern was heated in a large black tub over a fire. Smaller tubs were then filled with the hot water and soap. Ed and Howard scrubbed the clothes clean on washboards and rinsed them out in additional tubs. They even squeezed water out of the clothing by hand, until about 1940, when the family purchased a wringer machine.

E. F. Kruse believed that an idle mind is the devil's workshop. He thought his children needed to be busy. As if the chores at home weren't enough, Ed remembered delivering newspapers for a while. At one point, he offered to distribute circulars for a five-and-dime store. It took him five or six hours to roll and deliver them. Earning only 15 cents, he felt obligated to share a portion of his proceeds with the boy who got him the job.

As hard as Ed worked as a small boy, his life was spared the most devastating aspects of the Great Depression, which was occurring at that time. First, he lived in Brenham, a small town in Central Texas of about

6,000 people. Brenham was located on the Brazos River and was surrounded by vast amounts of fertile land. Townsfolk were able to purchase
food from farmers or grow it in their own backyards. Both of Ed's grand-
fathers, August Kruse and Henry Quebe, had emigrated from Germany
and had become very successful cotton and corn farmers in communities
near Brenham before their deaths in 1924 and 1925, respectively. All of their
children who survived to adulthood—seven on the Kruse side and nine
on the Quebe side—remained on farms in the area, with the exception of
Ed's parents. Even though they lived in town, the E. F. Kruse family would
never go hungry.

Second, E. F. had a somewhat secure position as the manager of Blue
Bell Creameries. However, the company definitely struggled during the
Depression. A decrease in profits resulted in lower wages for employees and eventually lower prices paid to farmers for their butterfat. E. F.
did not lay off any employees, but they worked strenuously to produce
butter and ice cream for consumers—overtime could mean 60, 70, or 80
hours per week. Even so, their pay remained the set amount the company
could afford to pay. Everyone at Blue Bell made it through the hard times
together.

One smart move E. F. made to boost income and help the company
remain in business was to open several Lotta Cream "stores." Located
inside other businesses, these dip stations allowed Blue Bell employees
to dish out double-dip ice cream cones to shoppers while they purchased
staples in town on Saturdays. At 5 cents per cone, the treat was a small
luxury people felt they could afford once a week. E. F. Kruse positioned
Lotta Cream stores inside Mr. Schmid's Savitall Grocery Store in Brenham and in other businesses in nearby towns like Giddings, Elgin, Taylor,
La Grange, Smithville, Bastrop, and Navasota. Blue Bell employees often
dipped as much as 120 gallons of ice cream on a Saturday.

The hard-working Kruses' main respite for the week was Sunday afternoons, after Sunday school and church. They usually drove out to one of
the uncles' farms. Ed remembered swimming and fishing in the creeks and
shooting his BB gun or slingshot at various targets with his cousins. They
played "cowboy" as they rode calves in the barn shed. Despite the fun, these
visits often entailed chores: Ed picked cotton, pulled corn, helped at the
cotton gin begun by Grandfather Quebe, and hand-milked cows in their
stalls.

Ed had particular admiration for his maternal grandfather, Henry
Quebe. Mr. Quebe started a new life in Central Texas after he arrived from
Germany as a young man. He prospered to such a degree that he developed

the habit of buying a farm, working hard until he paid it off, passing it over to a son as a wedding gift, and then moving to a new farm. He treated his daughters equally, gifting his daughter Bertha a house instead, since she and E. F. were going to be living in town.

Industriousness even found its way into Ed's recreational activities. His house had a huge yard adjoined by an empty lot, which was like a magnet to the older boys in the neighborhood. They played sandlot football, baseball, kickball, and every other sport imaginable. Although this was Ed's and Howard's home turf, the two young brothers were usually excluded when the actual games took place.

Ed recalled begging the older boys for opportunities to take a turn at bat, shag flies in the outfield, chase foul balls, act as referee, or participate in one way or the other. If they were shooting their BB guns, he wanted a chance to pull the trigger just once. Ed knew he had to prove himself if the older boys did allow him to play, so he practiced hard on his own, honed his skills, and became very competitive in all aspects of sports.

When the big boys weren't present, Ed, Howard, and their younger friends enjoyed making "rubber guns" using scrap wood, rubber from the inner tubes of damaged tires, and clothespins. Pressing the gun's clothespin would launch a rubber band at whatever target was in sight—sometimes a fellow playmate. (Even years later, Ed recalled how the "bullets" smarted!)

Ed and Howard also used old shoes and rubber from discarded inner tubes to make slingshots. Then Ed would walk the four blocks to the Farmers Merchants Lumber Yard to sift through the old gravel pit for the perfect round stones to use with their slingshots. Next the boys would set up an uneven number of tin cans on the top of their back fence. Each boy began shooting at a different end of the line and knocking the cans off in order. Whoever got to the middle can first (often an arguable point) and blasted it away won the game. The Kruse boys shot cans for hours at a time. They became proficient with their slingshots.

The one area in which Ed did not particularly apply himself was school. He made decent grades without much effort, which was okay with him. He adored his teachers at Alamo School—Miss Louise Giddings in first grade, Miss Ruth Hasskarl in second, Miss Lizzie Malsby in third, and Mrs. C. E. King in fourth—and did everything he could do to please them. He had no desire to be sent to the spooky cloakroom, nor did he relish the idea of his mother being invited to school to discuss a behavior problem.

Ed stated that he benefitted tremendously from the oral recitation his teachers required—reading aloud, participating in spelling bees, presenting book reports, reciting poetry, and sharing science and social studies projects. He also liked doing multiplication problems on the blackboard. The more active and competitive the activity, the more Ed favored it.

Ed attended Central School in fifth, sixth, and seventh grades, where he did get into trouble once with the principal, Mr. A. W. Shannon. It seems that Jimmie Bagley kept pinching Ed during an assembly. At recess, Ed challenged him to some "fisticuffs" and ended up giving Jimmie a black eye. Mr. Shannon reprimanded the boys and required them to report to his office after school for a period of time. Ed learned his lesson: he didn't get into any more fights. No doubt E. F. and Bertha Kruse supported Mr. Shannon's method of punishment and discussed with Ed better ways he could have used communication skills to deal with the pinching in the first place.

Ed's lack of top grades in school certainly did not reflect his parents' wishes or examples. E. F. Kruse not only went to Blinn College in Brenham after completing his education in the Rocky Hill schools near his boyhood home of Prairie Hill, but he also returned to Rocky Hill to teach. Feeling he needed additional training, E. F. completed a teaching course in San Marcos at Southwest Texas State Normal College (later known as Southwest Texas State Teachers College and now as Texas State University). He returned to his Rocky Hill students in 1917 and taught in the classroom until called to serve his country in World War I. When accepting the job

The children of E. F. and Bertha Kruse: Bertha and Mildred are standing behind Howard, Evelyn Ann, and Ed. Courtesy of Blue Bell Creameries

to become manager of the Brenham Creamery Company (later Blue Bell Creameries) in 1919, E. F. turned down an offer to be superintendent of the Burton School District. He obviously was recognized as an educated and esteemed citizen. Bertha, too, attended Blinn College to further the basic instruction she had received in the local schools.

Dinner table conversation at the Kruse home was filled with interesting topics to supplement the children's lessons from school. The seven Kruses said grace then launched into stories about activities at school and at Blue Bell. Living during the Depression and World War II, there were plenty of national and local news items to stimulate conversation.

One topic, which emerged several times, concerned sons who inherited their fathers' companies and, through neglect, greed, laziness, or poor business practices, bankrupted them. E. F. specified names and businesses so that Ed and Howard knew that he was not speaking hypothetically. E. F. never said that the boys should join Blue Bell on a full-time basis or that running the company would ever fall on their shoulders. But Ed and Howard got the point: if they were ever in a position to manage Blue Bell Creameries, they should be prepared and committed to work very diligently to continue its growth and success. Failure was not an option.

E. F. further used dinnertime as an opportunity to instill correct grammar habits. Detecting an error and acting as if he hadn't heard clearly, E. F. would say, "What was that?" Usually, the child repeated his or her statement and self-corrected the mistake. If not, E. F. would say an acceptable form of the word or phrase in a sentence himself, in hopes that the child would hear it correctly used. E. F. never openly criticized or embarrassed his children.

After dinner, the family sometimes gathered around their radio console to tune into their favorite program, "Dr. I. Q." Each of the Kruses competed to answer the challenging questions posed by "the doctor" to members of the audience in the Chicago Theater. The doctor offered silver dollars to his contestants for correct answers. Examples might be (1) $7 if the chosen person could tell which three states besides Texas bordered Mexico; (2) $6 to identify the capital of Pennsylvania; (3) $12 to differentiate between how a woman, a civilian man, and a soldier would honor the American flag as it passed during a parade; (4) $11 to state the name of the Secretary of the Communist Party in Russia; (5) $7 to identify the harbor in which the *U.S.S. Maine* sank; and (6) $25 to reveal the two first names of Colonel Goethals, who was the chief engineer of the Panama Canal. If the person did not answer the question correctly, the consolation prizes were two tickets to a production at the Chicago Theater and a box of twenty-four Milky Way Bars from the Mars Company, the sponsor of the show.

On other nights, the family might listen to musical programs featuring such acts as the Andrews Sisters, Rudy Valle and his Connecticut Yankees, or Bing Crosby. As pleasant as those family evenings were, Ed Kruse also enjoyed gatherings at friends' houses when he was about 12 years old. A particular game that boys and girls played involved walking a girl around the house and kissing her on the cheek. On his own twelfth birthday, Ed was particularly sweet on Joyce Kochwelp. Since it was his birthday and the party was at his house, he played "make a wish" and asked Joyce to walk around the house with him. That worked well, but by the end of the evening she was spending time with Bubba Schomburg. Not the best birthday! Discouraged but not defeated, Ed would play the game on other occasions with more success.

All of these learning experiences in the Kruse home were supplemented with carefully crafted family vacations, each with an instructive purpose in mind. One excursion took the Kruse family all the way to New Mexico and Carlsbad Caverns. On that trip, they also stopped in Del Rio and Uvalde. At the latter location, they stayed in Garner State Park and visited the home of Vice President John Nance Garner. Another adventure occurred in Hot Springs, Arkansas. As they drove, the family stopped at historical sites along the way and learned about various forms of flora and fauna. E. F., particularly, was always teaching but in subtle, enjoyable ways.

Ed recognized and appreciated the enriching benefits of these excursions, especially since so few people had the opportunity to travel during the Depression. Later, Ed would consciously plan similar enriching experiences for his own children.

Ed's favorite trips, however, were the short jaunts to the Gulf of Mexico to swim and, more important, to fish. Ed particularly treasured a fishing trip he and Howard took with their dad to the Texas Gulf Coast in 1940. A salesman friend of E. F.'s arranged the excursion since he knew more about mackerel fishing than E. F. did. Ed vividly recalled that the participants caught 105 mackerel, weighing between 1½ and 2 pounds each—details that a less competitive fisherman might not find important to remember.

On another occasion, the Kruse guys went trout fishing—an adventure that Ed enjoyed immensely. E. F. took his sons on other short fishing experiences and instilled in Ed a lifelong passion for the pastime. Ed appreciated his father's efforts, because he knew that E. F. didn't enjoy fishing nearly as much as Ed did.

Ed also fished at the Gun and Rod Club on the outskirts of town. He and Howard finished their chores as quickly as possible on summer days so that they could swim, fish, and shoot targets with their .22 rifles at this Brenham mainstay. Usually Ed pumped Howard on their one bicycle to get to the club, but sometimes their older sisters kindly dropped them off after lunch on their way back to their summer jobs at Blue Bell. The countless hours at the Gun and Rod Club were put to good use. Both boys became excellent swimmers, seasoned fishermen, and expert marksmen.

Ed learned additional skills in his Boy Scout troop. The scoutmaster was Sheriff Tieman H. Dippel Sr., who was a scout leader even before he had children of his own. The sheriff saw great value in the lessons of the Boy Scouts of America, and the program furnished a way for him to give back to his community.

Sheriff Dippel helped his scouts earn the typical merit badges in areas such as first aid, marksmanship, hiking, and woodcarving. Having access to the jail also provided him an opportunity to vary the experiences for his scouts. One of his favorite activities was to take a group of boys with him to the sheriff's office, talk to them about law enforcement, and show them the jail. When Ed's group went, Sheriff Dippel opened the door of the jailhouse, locked it behind him, and left the boys at the bottom of the two-story staircase while he went upstairs to make sure everything was all right. The sheriff finally told the boys it was safe for them to come up to tour the jail.

As they climbed the stairs, Ed heard a terrible groaning coming from one of the cells. Sheriff Dippel explained that he had captured the "Wild Man of Green Mountain" and was holding him until he could transfer him to an asylum in Austin. He allowed the boys to peer in at the prisoner through a small, barred opening in the steel door. The man growled at the boys menacingly. At that point, Sheriff Dippel unexpectedly was called to the phone and left the boys in the cell area. The captive became more agitated. One of the scouts even offered him a cigarette to calm him down—Ed cringed at the idea that it wasn't rare for a 12-year-old to have a cigarette in that day and age.

The wild man couldn't contain himself any longer; he leapt at the cell door—which flew open. He began chasing the boys down the stairs. The boys thought to run out the door at the bottom of the stairwell, but it was locked—they were trapped! If the Wild Man of Green Mountain hadn't burst out laughing, Sheriff Dippel probably would have rescued the boys in heroic style. As it turned out, the boys quickly realized they had been tricked and joined in the fun.

In another instance, Sheriff Dippel took his troops camping. The boys set up their cots over a wide area. Settling down for the night, they climbed into their sleeping bags and began talking loudly to each other and making lots of noise. Exhausted and needing sleep, Sheriff Dippel told the boys about the wolves who lived in the area and how they would pick off humans who seemed to be on their own. Gradually, the boys moved their cots closer to each other—and to Dippel. The sheriff assured them that the wolves probably wouldn't hurt them if they didn't attract too much attention. The boys got the message, quieted down, went to sleep, and lived to see another day.

Sheriff Dippel made a strong impression on young Ed. When he grew up, Ed Kruse became a scout leader. He wanted to impart the same educational, practical, and enjoyable activities to his sons and their friends that Sheriff Dippel had provided him. It gave Ed a great deal of pleasure to supervise Sheriff Dippel's son Skipper (Tieman H. Dippel Jr.) when the boy applied for his swimming and lifesaving merit badges.

With role models like Sheriff Dippel, Grandfather Quebe, his Kruse and Quebe uncles, and, especially, his father, Ed saw the benefits of hard work and its relationship to success from an early age. Observing is one thing; participating is another. Ed Kruse began preparing for a future career when he entered the workforce at age 13.

Answers to the Dr. I. Q. questions: (1) New Mexico, Arizona, and California; (2) Harrisburg; (3) a woman placed her right hand over her heart, a civilian man removed his hat and placed his hat over his heart, and a soldier saluted the flag; (4) Joseph Stalin; (5) Havana; (6) George Washington Goethals

Chapter Three

Be prepared.

• EDISM #25 •

IN 1941, ED KRUSE turned 13 years old, and already the halcyon days of his youth were behind him. E. F. decided that his sons needed to prepare for the real world. Beginning that June, he required Ed and Howard to work in the Blue Bell plant every summer, in the afternoons and on Saturdays during the school year, and throughout holiday vacations.

This was not an unprecedented move in the Kruse family. Older sisters Bertha and Mildred had been employed at Blue Bell for years during their off-school hours. What seems shocking is Ed's tender age of 13—that is, until we realize that in June 1941, his younger brother Howard had not yet reached his eleventh birthday.

In addition to his desire for his sons to establish a strong work ethic, E. F. may have actually needed their help. Despite the continuing economic woes of the country, an article in *The Hempstead News* in 1939 remarked upon the popularity of Blue Bell Ice Cream in the areas surrounding Brenham. (This included Hempstead, which was 22 miles to the east.) The reporter credited "the efficiency of [E. F.'s] management and the pleasing manner in which he conducts his business for the increasing range of the territory served by his company." The article further stated that the availability of refrigerated trucks allowed Blue Bell Ice Cream to be enjoyed up to 150 miles from the creamery. E. F.'s careful selection of ingredients and his close attention to the manufacturing process made it possible for the products to live up to the company's motto: "As Good As the Best, If Not Better."

For whatever reason E. F. had the young Kruse boys at the plant, he paid them for their work—10 cents per hour. During the summer, that

The original "Little Creamery in Brenham." Courtesy of Blue Bell Creameries

meant eight hours a day, six days a week. Each boy earned $4.80 per week. Of that amount, Ed and Howard divided their money in the same way: 5 cents went to Social Security (which was optional back then), their mother Bertha received $2.75 of their earnings for groceries and future educational expenses, and the boys were allowed to keep the remaining $2.00. Ed remarked that he spent his $2.00 quite freely, whereas Howard saved most of his earnings.

The boys' chores at the creamery varied greatly. For example, one task involved assembling ice cream sandwiches. After cutting a tray of solidly frozen vanilla ice cream into 64 four-ounce rectangular bars with a large knife, Ed and Howard placed each rectangle between two chocolate wafers and wrapped the sandwich in paper. They placed the sandwiches in boxes. Once filled, the boxes went back into the freezer to await distribution to customers. This job required strength and accuracy to slice through the frozen ice cream slab, dexterity to assemble each treat neatly, and speed to keep the ice cream from melting.

Sometimes the boys used the novelty tank to make ice cream bars on sticks. They worked with eight molds at a time. They filled the molds with soft ice cream via a funnel. A shortened broom handle helped them move the ice cream through the funnel into each mold. Afterward, the boys dipped the molds into a brine water solution until the ice cream inside the molds froze. At the proper stage of hardening, Ed and Howard inserted sticks into the ice cream. When the product was completely frozen, the boys placed the molds in hot water to loosen the novelties from the molds. At that point, they dipped the frozen treats into chocolate or some other coating, if required. Then they bagged and boxed the products by hand.

The boys didn't actually make ice cream, but they did prepare ingredients for the various flavors. They removed stems from juicy strawberries. They pulled ripe bananas off their stalks, peeled them, and mashed them for banana nut ice cream. Ed and Howard also cracked pecans and extracted the meat—carefully, without any pieces of shell. They pared fresh peaches, which was possibly the most unpleasant job of all. It wasn't difficult to take the skin off, but the fuzz stuck to the boys' skin in the heat of the summer and made them itch miserably.

Not everything Ed and Howard did involved frozen products. Blue Bell Creameries still made plenty of butter in 1941. E. F. often assigned the boys the task of wrapping pound and quarter-pound blocks of butter in paper and boxing them. The paper featured a pastoral scene of cows grazing in a meadow, along with the company's name. Ed and Howard had to wrap precisely so that the brand name lined up correctly on the stick of butter.

An arduous chore was washing the five-gallon metal cans that had been used to deliver ice cream to grocers. The cans came back to Blue Bell with

As boys, Ed and Howard Kruse wrapped many sticks of butter in papers such as this one. Courtesy of Blue Bell Creameries

remnants of melted ice cream stuck inside them. Often they had been sitting like that for a while—in the Texas heat—so the odor was unpleasant, to say the least. The boys would take the cans to the little wooden shack near the railroad tracks on the creamery property. Steam was piped into this building to make extremely hot water. Ed and Howard ran the hot water into the cans and scrubbed them thoroughly with a brush, then rinsed them completely. It was a job one could rightly take a great deal of pride in once it was done, but it was hot, difficult work.

Before accusing E. F. Kruse of abusing child labor laws, readers must keep in mind that Ed and Howard didn't do all these tasks as 13- and 11-year-olds. Nevertheless, they had a lot of responsibility for boys their age, and it only increased as they grew through their teens.

Ed knew that working at Blue Bell from an early age helped prepare him for his life ahead. He learned the ice cream and butter business from the bottom up. His dad helped him establish strong work habits and modeled leadership skills and ethical business practices for him. Young Ed also discovered the satisfaction of earning his own money and, at the same time, giving back to his family. These lessons would pay off in countless ways in the future.

One of the books that Ed recommended to friends of all ages is *Naya Nuki, Shoshoni Girl Who Ran* by Kenneth Thomasma. Even though it's written at a sixth-grade reading level, the story focuses on an important message: being prepared. Eleven-year-old Naya and her friend Sacajawea were kidnapped by members of the Minnetare tribe and marched 1,000 miles from southwestern Montana to a village in North Dakota, where they became slaves.

From the very moment she was captured, Naya meticulously planned her escape. She worked constantly to accomplish her goal—watching the landscape as she traveled, making extra pairs of moccasins, storing away food, pilfering items to help her survive, and patiently watching for her opportunity.

When the right time came, Naya set off toward home. Eluding would-be captors, escaping bears, avoiding freezing to death, nursing herself through a serious illness, and following the lessons she had so carefully learned, Naya returned safely to her mother and her tribe. Naya triumphed over crushing adversity through preparation and fortitude.

The hardships that Ed and Howard faced working in the plant were not nearly so difficult as those confronting Naya, but all three youngsters benefited from thinking ahead and getting ready for whatever came next. However, unlike Naya, the Kruse boys and others whom E. F. hired during the summer also managed to have fun despite the work involved. For example, the youngsters took advantage of the ice that accumulated on the pipes through which the ice cream mix flowed. They scraped the ice off the pipes and engaged in lively snowball fights.

In another case, Ed and his friend Tony Zientek were wrapping butter when some accidentally flipped off Ed's fingers and hit Tony in the face. Tony retaliated by flicking some butter off his knife in Ed's direction. Before long, a full-scale butter battle was taking place. Ed recalled that Tony "started running out the door, and I had a handful of butter in hot pursuit. Little did I know until too late that my father was right behind me. Dad took me to a red storage building outside, removed his belt, and I got a good spanking. Needless to say, that never happened again." E. F. didn't mind the boys enjoying their work, but wasting product was a different matter.

Being the boss, E. F. undoubtedly held his own sons to a higher standard than other employees. He ran a tight ship in any case. For example, he never cursed. Ed and Howard claimed that the words "hell" or "damn" never passed their father's lips. If E. F. heard someone swearing in the plant, he approached the guilty party and asked if using that language contributed to better performance on the job. Of course, the answer was, "No, sir." Having butter fights also fell into the category of unacceptable behavior.

In those early days of working at the creamery, Ed and Howard rode their one bike to and from work. Ed pumped Howard on the handlebars or fender. They had an hour off for lunch, so they made a round trip home to eat. After the boys left the plant for the day, they climbed on their bike and rode home.

Having a paying job was not the only new experience for Ed in 1941. The Kruse family moved into a different house. Having their original house placed on rollers and moved to the empty lot next door, the Kruses built a new home on their old site.

Only the immediate E. F. Kruse family would reside in the new home. All the tenants renting apartments from the Kruse family remained in the original house, and Bertha Schlottmann Quebe, who had lived with her daughter's family for several years, died in June 1941 at the age of 86. Her death was a sad, growing-up experience for young Ed. He remembered Grandma Quebe rocking him as a boy in the family rocking chair, which is now in his family's home. She told him stories of taking food and water to the workers at her father's cotton gin, as well as that of her husband. She also related tales of her midwifery days in the Cedar Hill community. Ed felt a very close bond to Grandma Quebe.

In addition to extra space in the house on South Austin Street, the Kruses experienced more amenities. For example, the house had central heating, though no central air-conditioning. Everything seemed fresh and modern compared to the old house. The two-story brick house had three bedrooms: one for E. F. and Bertha, one for the three girls, and one for Ed and Howard. Even though the boys had two double beds in their room, they often slept together in one because they were so accustomed to it.

One of the nice features of the new house was a sun deck. It often became a sleeping porch during the hot Brenham summers. The bedroom Ed and Howard shared was on the west side of the house, so their room heated up in the afternoons. To make matters worse, the prevailing breeze from the southeast didn't come at a proper angle to cool off that part of the house. Often in the middle of the night, the bedraggled boys would lug their bedding through their parents' room and set up camp on the sun deck. E. F. would protest—saying it really wasn't that hot. However, sometimes when the boys awoke in the mornings, E. F. would be sleeping on the porch with them.

Starting work at Blue Bell and moving into the new house made 1941 a special year for 13-year-old Ed Kruse. He certainly could have done without the third memorable milestone. On December 7, 1941—Franklin Delano Roosevelt's "date which will live in infamy"—the Japanese bombed Pearl Harbor in Hawaii. Ed clearly remembered Mrs. Byrd running out of the upstairs apartment in the rental house and shouting the news. Ed wasn't sure how this national crisis would change his life, but he was ready to do his part.

Chapter Four

You can whip almost any problem
if you work hard enough and long enough.

• EDISM #5 •

IN ORDER TO STRIKE BACK at Emperor Hirohito for the surprise attack on Pearl Harbor and to reverse Adolph Hitler's efforts to take over Europe, the United States declared war. Consequently, every American was expected to work hard and long to conquer the country's foes. Ed Kruse was no exception. Meanwhile, he needed to help his dad keep Blue Bell Creameries afloat and, at the same time, try to live a somewhat normal life during his high school years, which coincided directly with America's participation in World War II.

The first order of business for the country was to retool for the war effort. For example, all of the automakers stopped manufacturing new cars and made airplanes, trucks, and tanks for the military instead. Similarly, factories switched to producing firearms, ammunition, uniforms, and essential equipment for the soldiers. Rationing took effect and left civilians short of gasoline, tires, coffee, cars, dairy products, sugar, and many other everyday commodities.

In Brenham, E. F. Kruse became head of the draft board for Washington County and made sure that men whose national lottery numbers were chosen reported to their respective divisions of the armed services. Blue Bell geared up to produce railcar loads of butter for the American troops, such as those stationed at Fort Hood in nearby Killeen, Texas. The company continued to make ice cream, but it was often a very poor product, depending on which ingredients were available: lard, black strap molasses, powdered milk, honey, dark Karo syrup, and vegetable oil did not compare to the fresh cream and sugar available before the war.

This page from the 1945 *Brenhamite* shows Ed Kruse as president of the senior class. Other officers are James Hay, vice president; Sarah Holle, secretary; Betty Sloan, representative; and Carl Schomburg, representative. Courtesy of Ed. F. and Evelyn Kruse and the 1945 *Brenhamite*

Ed was always embarrassed by the substandard ice cream that Blue Bell manufactured during World War II. He wondered if his dad should have made fewer but better products, rather than continuing to increase sales. Ed felt that it took a long time for Blue Bell to regain consumers' confidence in the quality of its ice cream again. In any case, Ed learned an important lesson: quality would remain supreme under his future management.

Of course some of the most valuable Blue Bell employees joined the armed services. Those left behind were under 17, older than 36, or classified as 4-F, which meant they had health conditions unacceptable for the draft. Just as during the Great Depression, no one was laid off at Blue Bell during the war. Those employees who stayed worked arduously between 50 and 80 hours each week to keep the business running as smoothly as possible. Their earnings were capped—from $15 to $25 per week—due to regulations set by the US Salary Stabilization Unit.

Everyone had to pitch in. On many nights, the entire Kruse family went to the plant to make frozen novelties for salesman Andy Anderson to deliver on his route the next morning, providing Blue Bell had the tires and gasoline necessary for him to perform his job.

Because of their youth, Ed and most of his contemporaries did not serve in the armed services. Instead, they supported the war effort through purchasing war bonds; recycling tin, rubber, and newspapers; helping with Victory Gardens; participating in "meatless" Tuesdays; and writing to servicemen overseas.

They also strived to live ordinary teenage lives under abnormal circumstances, which basically meant attending high school. Ed walked or rode his bicycle to Brenham High School, which was located on South Market Street. Built in 1928, it featured a cafeteria, an auditorium, and a brand-new native-rock gymnasium, which had been constructed under the auspices of

President Franklin Roosevelt's Works Progress Administration. A football field adjoined the site. The athletic facilities supported games played by the Brenham High School Cubs, whose colors were green and white.

The school held grades 8 through 11. Each of the freshman, sophomore, junior, and senior classes had between 70 and 100 students, with Ed's class of 1945 consisting of 73 students. Ed eventually graduated in the top 25 percent of his class, making As and Bs without too much effort. Had he a chance to do it all over again, Ed stated he would have applied himself more. The intelligence was there; the gung-ho attitude was not. As it was, he performed well enough academically: his overall high school average was in the 87 to 88 percent range, with science, math, and English as his favorite subjects. He did not take a foreign language.

Each day of Ed's high school schedule was divided into six classes. Free periods were spent in the library. After doing homework, Ed enjoyed using his spare time to read the Boys Allies series. It concerned two American boys, Frank Chadwick and Jack Templeton, who met each other shortly after the declaration of World War I. Aboard the British cruiser *Sylph*, the boys took off for many adventures—at Verdun, in the Balkan campaign, at Jutland, and with the Russian Cossacks. With World War II going on around him, Ed found inspiration and patriotism in these accounts.

Some of Ed's most remarkable mentors were Miss Beatrice Slagle, his English teacher; Miss Wilson, who taught him science; Mr. Frank W. Allenson, his physics instructor; Mr. John Laguinn Buckley, the principal of Brenham High School; Miss Eunice Brackett; and Jordice Park. Years later, Ed ran into Miss Slagle (then Mrs. Beatrice Wiese) at a high school reunion and told her he greatly appreciated having her as a teacher. With tears in her eyes, she thanked Ed and expressed how much it would have meant to hear it from him as a student. Ed must have been a typical teenager; he didn't realize how much he had gained from his high school teachers until later in life.

Ed did learn from this interaction with his former teacher, however. He encouraged groups of students to whom he spoke to thank the teachers who had already made a difference in their lives. Ed himself was always quick to voice appreciation to those who helped him—in person, by phone, or through his prompt and sincere thank-you notes.

Although he admired and wanted to emulate many of his instructors, Ed respected his coach Owen Erekson the most. He was the person who inspired Ed to work hard in practice and to use psychology in preparing for games. He refined Ed's leadership skills and provided opportunities for him to use them. Coach Erekson trusted Ed to call all the plays as quarterback—an opportunity that Ed relished and an experience that pre-pared him for his future career. Coach also emphasized the importance of teamwork, a defining theme in Ed's life.

Ed used Coach Erekson's preparation for the Cubs' football game against the Smithville Tigers in his senior year to demonstrate why he held the coach in such high esteem. At that time, Coach explained that their opponents didn't have a very good squad, except for one huge guy named Skinner. Skinner was going to play over the Cubs center, and his usual ploy was to beat up on that player and wear him down. So Coach Erekson designed a play called the Skinner Special, to get Skinner thinking right.

Ed quoted Coach Erekson's terse instructions: "So, Kruse, you're going to take the ball from center, and Gaskamp, as right halfback, you're going to run right over the center and step on Skinner. Sommer, I want you to do the same thing, and Haack, I want you to do the same thing. And Kruse, you keep the ball and run over him too."

When Ed called the play, it went as planned, although he never remember even seeing Skinner during the process. All he knew was that after that play, Skinner could not have been more gentlemanly. He repeatedly picked up Cubs off the ground and told them, "Good play." The Cubs won 59–0.

E. F. Kruse also used that game as a coaching opportunity. Due to a rainstorm and a detour, Ed reached home at 3 a.m. following the Cubs' win over the Smithville Tigers. He hoped his father would allow him to sleep in and not work at the plant that day. When he heard his father leave at 7:30 a.m. for the office, he snuggled back under his covers and figured he had the day to himself. Arising at 8 a.m., Ed went downstairs to breakfast and was informed by his mother that he was expected at Blue Bell at 9 o'clock. E. F. Kruse didn't leave his children much time to get into trouble.

With Coach Erekson as an inspiration, it's no wonder Ed went out for football, basketball, and track during his high school years. In the end, all those hours of practicing and aspiring to play with the older boys in his backyard had paid off: Ed's athletic skills made him very competitive. Ed confessed that his main focus in high school was sports, even to the extent of daydreaming about upcoming games during academic classes.

In football, he played quarterback and lettered in his junior and senior years—those were the days of leather helmets and no faceguards. Ed also played secondary on defense. As a senior, he was co-captain of the football team. With a record of eight wins and two losses, the Brenham Cubs won the District 33A championship title.

When the team advanced to the regional game against the El Campo

Rice Birds, the program described #55 "Edward Kruse" as "148 lb. 16-year-old. 1 letter. Senior. Smooth handler. Flashy runner. Excellent punter and passer. Has developed into a smart signal caller and safety. One of the best ball handlers ever seen in high school circles."

Unfortunately, the Cubs lost the regional game to the Rice Birds, but the *Brenham Banner-Press* proclaimed, "The Cubs came through the season in fine style doing much more than most people expected of them.... They played their hearts out to win."

Ed also played on the Brenham High School basketball team for three years. He lettered during his junior and senior years and served as co-captain as a senior. That team went on to win the district championship.

Positioned as a guard, Ed consistently scored in the double digits—often the most points in the game. In fact, the Cubs lost a game to Bellville early in Ed's senior season, 19–8. Tommy Blake, the sports reporter for the *Brenham Banner-Press*, noted Ed's absence and its effect on the game: "Edward Kruse, stellar little hustler for the Brenham team, was missing from the game due to illness, and the Cub floor game was nothing. Kruse took ill Friday afternoon and was not allowed to make the trip. Had he been in the lineup, it may have been a different ball game."

The Cubs won their District 25A basketball title but lost in the regional tournament. The San Antonio Sidney Lanier Voks topped the Brenham Cubs by a score of 35 to 28. It may have been some consolation to Ed and his teammates to know that they had lost to the state champs. Lanier went on to beat Quitman 30–24 for the Texas Class 1A title.

In addition, Ed joined the track team, partly because he simply enjoyed being with his friends. It also excused him from after-school duties at the creamery. Ed knew he was not a gifted runner. The idea of his going out for the 100-yard dash or even the 220 made no sense. He chose to compete in the half-mile race. Because of his hard work and determination, Ed outlasted most of the other runners and ended up placing third in district in his senior year.

Another example of Ed's competitiveness occurred at a track meet in Giddings. Ed did his part for the Cubs by coming in third in the 880-yard race. Afterward, Ed pondered the fact that Brenham had no one to enter the pole vault event—actually, Brenham High School didn't even have a pole-vault pit. Ed's thought was: How hard could it be? So he talked his friends Robert Gaskamp and Ben Wehring into entering the competition with him.

Both Ed and Robert failed three times to make it over the eight-foot bar—the lowest height. Ben, who was small, wiry, and fast, managed to clear the crossbar at 10 feet and won second place for that event. Ed admitted that the additional points didn't cause Brenham High School to take home the first-place trophy (the Cubs actually came in second), but he was pleased that he and his friends had challenged themselves and added to the Cubs' overall score.

Coach Erekson was so impressed with Ed's enthusiasm, work ethic, and sports skills that he came up with a plan for Ed to play for the Brenham Cubs for an additional semester. The idea was that Ed would take chemistry from Coach in his senior year and earn an "incomplete"; then Ed would have to return the following fall to pass the course. According to Coach, while he was there, he might as well quarterback the football team again! Ed never considered the offer. Integrity was important to him even at that young age. He was flattered but said "no, thank you" to the proposition.

There was life outside of Blue Bell, sports, and studies when Ed attended high school. For example, he treasured and enjoyed his many lifelong friendships. Like the other kids, Ed went home for lunch almost every day, but they all made it back to school in time to play horseshoes before afternoon classes began. On rare occasions, his entire group would go to the Green Valley Restaurant for lunch. The 15-cent meal included a hot dog, potato chips, and a drink. Another nickel would buy some time on the pinball machine. The device sometimes got hung up and offered free games. One lunchtime Robert Gaskamp and Ed won 96 free games. Instead of going back to school, Robert opted to skip his afternoon classes and continue playing. He dutifully promised Ed that he would save a few games for him. After school ended at 3:40, Ed hurried over to the Green Valley Restaurant, where Robert was just completing the last game.

The only time Ed skipped school himself was on a warm February day during his senior year in 1945. The temperatures hovered in the 80 to 85 degree range. New Year's Creek beckoned Ed and his friends to swim. They followed temptation and swam to their hearts' content. Of course the hard part came when Ed had to forge a note from his father—and sign it. Doing so made Ed extremely nervous; in fact, he was pretty much on pins and needles all day—which negated some of the fun. He never played hooky again.

Despite his father's displeasure, sometimes Ed managed to slip off to a pool parlor with his friends. It cost a nickel a stick to play pool. The loser of the match paid a dime for both sticks. Ed didn't have much spare money for pool, so he had to hone his skills on the spot or he couldn't afford to play at all.

Ed never settled down with one girl in high school. He would date someone a few times and then switch to someone else. The two prettiest girls in high school were Sarah Carolyn Holle, in his own class, and Carolyn Miller, in the class behind him. He liked them and a number of other girls as well.

For the most part, the teens ran around in groups of boys and girls. They would go over to one of their homes and listen to music on the radio. Favorite country and Western singers were Eddie Arnold, Bob Wills and his Texas Playboys, Ernest Tubb, and Red Foley.

One special night that Ed never forgot was his seventeenth birthday. His family and friends had planned a surprise party for him. Three couples started out on a triple date: with gas rationing, people had to squeeze together in one car. Ed was particularly happy to have Bobbie Jo Schwernemann sitting on his lap. Bubba Schomburg just *happened* to remember that he had to run by Ed's house to pick up something for Luther League, a church youth organization. Ed remained in the car with Bobby Jo. Bubba came to the front door and yelled to Ed that he had a phone call. Not eager to remove Bobbie Jo from his lap, Ed asked Bubba to take a message. Bubba insisted that Ed come to the phone. When he walked

Ed Kruse is shown here with Carolyn Miller. The two were voted Mr. and Miss Popularity by their fellow students. Courtesy of Ed. F. and Evelyn Kruse and the 1945 *Brenhamite*

in the door, everyone shouted, "Surprise!" It was a memorable occasion—featuring a scavenger hunt, horseshoes, games on the porch, and plenty of tasty snacks.

The surprise party was on March 15, 1945. A mere two months later, Ed graduated from Brenham High School. He had worked hard and accomplished much. In addition to his leadership positions and victorious sports seasons, he served as president of both his freshman and senior classes; he participated in the student council; and the student body named him "Mr. Popularity" during his senior year.

Ed was basically a clean-cut, red-blooded American boy in high school—one who toed the line, thanks to the examples and expectations of his parents. He felt very fortunate to have grown up in the small community of Brenham and to have weathered the Great Depression and World War II surrounded by a close, loving family and lifelong friends. Despite its decided advantages, however, his sheltered life did not quite prepare him for what came next.

Chapter Five

Set goals and work toward them.

• EDISM #33 •

TO LEAVE A LOVING, calm home and arrive as a freshman on the campus of Texas A&M University was about as much of a culture shock as any young man could experience. First, Ed Kruse was the only student from Brenham at Texas A&M, so initially he knew no one on campus. Second, being in an all-male environment and belonging to the Corps of Cadets brought a number of additional surprises.

Ed was the only undergraduate from Brenham because most of the young men in the high school classes above him had joined the war effort and not gone to college. When Ed graduated from Brenham High School in May 1945, Germany had already surrendered, but the war against Japan was still being waged. Many of the boys from Ed's high school class opted to go into the armed services to help bring that theater of the war to a close. Those who chose to continue their education usually attended Blinn College, right there in Brenham. Others had to go immediately into the workforce or help on their family farms.

Ed had known for many years that he wanted to attend a four-year university. He did not cherish the learning so much as he felt that a college degree would help him get somewhere in life. His parents, strong proponents of higher education, encouraged Ed's decision. Ed's older sisters, Bertha and Mildred, had completed the two-year program at Blinn College, but Ed wanted to do more. His goal was to be the first in his family to achieve a university degree.

Texas A&M was the logical choice for Ed for several reasons. The campus was only 39 miles away, and, because gasoline rationing was still a factor, it made sense to be close to home.

In addition, Texas A&M offered a degree in dairy manufacturing, which was the course of study most interesting to Ed. He had grown up at Blue Bell Creameries and could see himself continuing in the dairy business in one form or another. The only other choice for a dairy manufacturing degree was Texas Tech University in Lubbock, which was about 450 miles away and not amenable to traveling back home on weekends. Ed had also considered becoming a preacher or teacher along the way, but finally he decided on a career in the dairy industry.

At Texas A&M at that time, freshmen automatically joined the Corps of Cadets. Ed figured that if the academics were too distasteful or difficult for him and he lasted only a year or two, he would still have enough college and military background to possibly qualify for Officers Candidate School. If Ed actually stayed the entire four years and graduated, he would enter the army as a second lieutenant and possibly pursue a military career.

Ed was basically paying for his college education with money he had earned from working at Blue Bell. Although E. F. supplemented funds when necessary, Ed faced a very tight budget. Attending a nearby university, where uniforms were provided, helped save money.

Ed Kruse arrived on the Texas A&M campus in College Station in the fall of 1945. He moved into Dorm 12 and was placed into B Troop Cavalry in the Aggie Corps of Cadets. That outfit occupied the third and fourth floors of Dorm 12. B Troop Cavalry had a number of sophomores, a few juniors, and several seniors, in addition to the lowly freshmen, who were referred to as "fish." In total, there were about seventy-five people in the unit. The commanding officer was Chester Reed, for whom Reed Arena—Texas A&M's basketball and all-purpose center—is named, and Ronald Reger was the top kick (i.e., first sergeant).

Even though he was the only student from Brenham, it did not take Ed long to begin meeting people. Being required to memorize the name, major, and hometown of every person in B Troop Cavalry aided that process. If introduced to a person outside of his unit, he also had to learn the same information—and repeat it at the request of any punitive upperclassman. Ed figured that by the end of his freshman year, he knew about 4,500 of the approximately 5,000 students on campus.

Acquiring such information was a method of hazing at Texas A&M. There were other mild forms, such as not being able to sit on your bed from 7 a.m. to 11 p.m. Freshmen wore a white stripe on their uniforms to distinguish them from upperclassmen. They were required to make up their beds so tightly that a quarter could bounce on it. Walking on sidewalks was disallowed; freshmen trudged through the gutters. Every upperclassman was addressed with "Yes, sir" or "No, sir." Standing at attention before marching formally into mess hall was expected, and freshmen never sat down at a football or baseball game.

The freshmen also had to know all the buildings on campus, their purposes, and for whom they were named. In addition, they memorized all the statues and the inscriptions on them. The rest of his life Ed Kruse could state, "Lawrence Sullivan Ross, 1838–1898, Soldier, Statesman, Knightly Gentleman, Brigadier General Confederate States of America, President of Texas A&M University." Ed felt that this mental hazing was actually good for him—he met people, became immersed in university traditions, and sharpened his memorization skills. Learning to pay attention to the personal details of new acquaintances proved to be a decided asset in the real world.

What he was not prepared for was the "board." This harsh form of hazing, which consisted of vicious paddling on the buttocks, was introduced to the freshmen after about two weeks on campus. Totally appalled, Ed wondered what he had gotten himself into. Unfortunately for him, B Troop Cavalry was particularly notorious for this practice. On one unforgettable occasion, Ed's rear end was so bruised that he showed Howard when he was home that weekend so that his little brother could learn what awaited him if he went to Texas A&M. He had to make Howard promise not to tell their mother. Ed saw no purpose in this cruelty and never used it on freshmen when he was an upperclassman. He felt luckier than most. He was athletic and in good condition. He had a strong will. No one was going to break him.

When Ed attended a baseball game as a freshman, some of the upperclassmen required him to chew a cigar and not spit out the tobacco juice. Swallowing made him extremely nauseated. Consequently, he decided to stay away from the baseball field for the rest of that spring.

Another culture shock involved the amount of bad language used by Corps members. Ed came from a home with strong Christian values. No one uttered curse words. There was a sense of proper decorum in his family, and Ed had attended church every Sunday. He was completely unprepared for the amount of offensive language he encountered in college. To quote Ed, "It was quite a rude awakening when the pissheads (sophomores) got hold of me as a freshman."

The excess drinking surprised him too. Ed came from a German community where a good beer was appreciated. Nevertheless, the drinking at

A&M got out of hand when cadets became drunk and disorderly. Ed wasn't tempted to drink much in college because he didn't have spare money to spend. Besides, he could only tolerate two beers at one time when he did drink.

Facing these startling changes to his life, Ed was not alone in his misery. He bonded closely to his roommates and other freshmen in his unit. They developed a strong camaraderie through experiencing their freshman year in the Corps of Cadets together. Decades later, freshmen roommates Gene Lehmann from Kerrville and Faburn "Frog" Murray from El Campo still drove to Brenham, spent the night at his house, and attended the Texas A&M versus LSU football game with Ed every time it was played in College Station. Other close classmates from his class of 1949 included the late Johnson D. "Shady" Strickel; Jim Nelson, with whom Ed received the Distinguished Alumnus Award in 2005; Clifford A. Taylor, a fellow member of the Advisory Council for the George Herbert Walker Bush School of Government and Public Service; Bernard Syfan, an Aggie swim team member; Philip McDaniel; and the late Mermod Jaccard. All of them suffered together the command, "Hit a brace, freshman!" (i.e., stand at rigid attention).

Despite these distractions in college, Ed managed to study hard. He often commented that a similar work ethic in high school would have resulted in straight As. Ed's grades at Texas A&M were good, although he often jokes that it took him six tries to get through organic chemistry. He actually passed it the first time around and was even exempted from the final exam, but it stood out to him as a really tough course.

Ed enjoyed reminiscing about the Corps of Cadets and academics at Texas A&M, but his favorite topic of conversation about his college years concerned sports. He remained a competitor and hated the thought of giving up athletic participation.

His greatest desire would have been to walk onto the football team. To do that, he had to weigh at least 200 pounds or run 100 yards in 10 seconds flat. Even at 5' 11" Ed entered Texas A&M weighing 148 pounds. In fact, he never in his life approached the 200-pound mark. Playing Aggie football was not an option.

Ed actually made the basketball squad, but in the process of practicing with the team, he severely pulled a leg muscle. He was injured to the point that he could barely stand up. While he was recuperating, an upperclassman, "Mr." Nelson from Galveston, suggested that he try to make the swimming team.

Nelson knew that Ed had placed first in a 100-yard freestyle event in the intramurals swim meet. In doing so, Ed had beat two of the members

Ed Kruse participated on the swimming team at Texas A&M University. Courtesy of Ed. F. and Evelyn Kruse

of the A&M swim team. Ed took Nelson's advice and went to talk to swimming coach Art Adamson. The first thing Coach Adamson asked about was Ed's limp. Ed explained that he had injured himself in basketball practice. Coach Adamson demanded, "If you swim, you don't play anything else." Then he suggested that Ed return when the limp was completely gone.

It took six weeks for Ed to be able to walk normally. When he went back to the P. L. Downs Natatorium, Coach Adamson asked what made him think he could swim. Ed explained to him about the intramural victory, so Coach told him to put on a swimsuit. He gave Ed a tryout and then welcomed Ed to the team. Ed would be on the team for more than three years and letter in his senior year.

The three hours of swim practice every day plus his rigorous coursework and the Corps requirements made for a busy schedule. In addition, Ed enjoyed playing intramural fast-pitch softball. Nevertheless, he learned to manage his time well and delighted in being part of the athletic program at Texas A&M.

One decided advantage of his new status on the swim team was his ability to live in the athletic dorm—Hart Hall—at Texas A&M. That switch took place midway through his sophomore year. It also meant that he got to eat heartily at the training table at Sbisa Mess Hall for seven months of the year. In addition, Ed's position in the Corps of Cadets changed: he became part of the B Athletics outfit. The A Athletics unit contained all the football players, whereas B Athletics included the track and swim team members and tennis players. Everyone in an athletics unit was in ROTC and an officer.

Moreover, athletics proved to be a broadening experience for Ed Kruse. He traveled widely as a member of the Texas A&M swim team. He went to meets at the campuses of the Southwest Conference schools in Austin, Dallas, Houston, Waco, Fort Worth, and Fayetteville, Arkansas. He also traveled to competitions in Oklahoma and Kansas. Detroit, Michigan, was his destination for the national water-polo championships in the summer of 1948: Ed played goalie for the team.

In fact, these are the travels that produced one of the major lessons in Ed's life. When his dad discovered Ed had been taking a towel from each hotel where the Aggie swim team stayed, he reminded Ed that "No one gets lost on a straight road." Ed always appreciated the fact that his dad caught him, made him send the towels back with notes of apology, and taught him a lesson that invaluably influenced his life.

When Ed didn't have weekend swimming responsibilities, he hitch-hiked home to Brenham. For the most part, he did not have a hard time finding transit. It was very common to see Aggies in uniform hitchhiking, and drivers were quick to pick them up. Sometimes on weekends, there would be as many as twenty Aggies lined up in front of the College Station Administration Building at A&M trying to catch a ride home. Ed just had to wait his turn.

While in Brenham, he caught up with family and friends, helped out at Blue Bell, and ate some much-appreciated home cooking. He also used these opportunities to advise Howard on how to avoid hazing if he decided to attend Texas A&M University. As it turned out, one of the mothers of a student in B Troop Cavalry found out about the extent of the hazing taking place and complained to the administration. The solution was to move all the freshmen to a dorm at Bryan Air Force Base. They were transported in buses to campus for their classes.

Ed watched this situation carefully and felt that the change made the hazing situation worse for freshmen rather than better. He therefore encouraged Howard to go out for freshman football so that he could live in the athletic dorm. Howard followed Ed's advice, and when he entered A&M in 1948, he had a much easier time. Howard not only dodged the hassle of upperclassmen's demands and the painful "board," he had time to study and make outstanding grades.

Despite the cruel beatings, the shame of being constantly chewed out, and the physically strenuous demands from the upperclassmen, Ed felt that he benefited from his freshman experience. According to him, if you could get through that first year at Texas A&M, you could face almost anything life held in store. There would be instances in Ed's future that were really tough to handle, but he knew he wouldn't run away. He could stand up to adversity and not just survive but thrive.

When Ed became an upperclassman, he refused to lord over or "swing a board" on a freshman. He left the new recruits alone for the most part.

The only time he bothered an underclassman was when the younger fellow allowed his grades to drop. Ed felt it was appropriate for him to step in at that point and remind the student of why he was at school in the first place.

Ed didn't date much in college. The most obvious reason was that there were no women in the Texas A&M student body at the time. If a boy wanted a girl to come to campus for a weekend or a special occasion, he had to pay for her transportation and her lodging in a motel or boarding house. Ed did not have spare funds for that purpose, nor did he have the time—especially because he spent most weekends at home. Ed didn't even call girls on the phone. He knew there must have been a telephone somewhere in his dorm, but he never needed to use it.

Being in athletics helped defray some of the college expenses for Ed, but he continued to need money from his summer work at Blue Bell to pay for tuition and board. As he grew older, his tasks varied. At the creamery, he helped make frozen treats, processed fruit, wrapped butter, and did many of the chores he learned as a boy. He also started to help manufacture ice cream and churn butter. He performed butterfat tests in the office and learned to read them. When farmers brought butterfat to the creamery, Ed calculated their cash proceeds. He even delivered ice cream with Blue Bell veteran Andy Anderson, substituted on other routes, and eventually ran routes himself.

His most memorable event from that period occurred when Andy Anderson was ill and Ed had to run a route solo. His mission was to drive out to Eagle Lake in a two-speed truck that had real problems climbing hills. The deliveries took much longer than he planned. Some of the ice cream was soft by the time he reached its destination. To make matters worse, three of his customers had closed by the time he arrived at their stores. One angry grocery store owner chewed him out in front of a crowd coming out of a movie theatre. How

Ed Kruse's senior photograph at Texas A&M University. Courtesy of Blue Bell Creameries

dare he deliver soft ice cream! Ed felt totally humiliated. Nothing an Aggie upperclassman could have done to him compared to the shame he felt at letting his father down on his first trial route.

The incident with the foiled route was truly atypical of Ed Kruse. He excelled across the board at Texas A&M. He lettered in swimming his senior year, and the team finished second in the medley relay in the Southwest Conference, where Ed placed fourth in the 150-yard backstroke. Ed also served as the executive officer of B Athletics in his senior year. In addition, he received a reserve commission in the Army in the armored (tank) division. Another very proud moment occurred when Ed was named a distinguished military student. All paled in comparison, however, to his receiving a bachelor of science degree in dairy manufacturing from Texas A&M University in May 1949. He had achieved his goal.

As the graduation kudos faded, Ed realized that he needed to decide which step he would take next toward his future.

Chapter Six

Think ahead.

• EDISM #32 •

ED HAD ALREADY ASSUMED that he would spend at least two years in the US Army, because that's what graduates from Texas A&M committed to do. In May 1949, Ed went to Fort Hood in Killeen, Texas, for summer training. Once again, he excelled in sports. After winning two swimming events and playing on the championship baseball team, Ed received special recognition by the regular Army captain as the outstanding athlete in his company.

That successful introduction to the armed forces was most encouraging. However, Congress was in a budget crunch. After all, World War II had been over for four years and the Korean conflict was not yet on the horizon. In May 1949, Congress announced that it would not automatically take officers directly out of Texas A&M. Instead, the Army would accept only those young graduates who volunteered for a full military career.

Ed Kruse considered that option. The thought of serving for 20 years and then retiring as a lieutenant colonel at the age of 41 was enticing, but there were many drawbacks. For example, one moved often in the Army. Such disruption would be detrimental to the family he hoped to have. In addition, Ed wondered if he were cut out for all the Army protocol and formal socializing. Although he felt he could certainly handle that aspect of military life, it did not particularly appeal to him. The deciding factor was that his country simply did not need his service at that time. It seemed more beneficial to put his dairy manufacturing degree to work. Ed declined his active Army commission but remained in the Army reserves.

A logical next move for Ed would be to return to Brenham and work for Blue Bell Creameries. The problem was that E. F. Kruse had expected

Ed to be in the Army for two years, so there was no position for him at the company. Ed needed to look elsewhere.

The head of the dairy science department at Texas A&M suggested Ed consider Swift and Company's Dairy and Poultry Division. At the time, Swift, a corporation known for its meat processing and sales, was also the fourth largest manufacturer of ice cream in the United States. After Ed interviewed for a position and achieved the highest score in Swift's history on the employment test, T. L. Sandlin hired him as an outside ice cream salesman and sent him to Fort Worth, Texas.

Before Ed left Brenham to begin his new job, E. F. surprised him one evening by hinting that he go out to the driveway. Sitting there was a brand-new 1949 Chevrolet. E. F. gave him the keys, and Ed drove it around the block a few times. E. F. then took Ed to his desk and had him sign a $2,000 note with 5 percent interest. Ed could not have been more thrilled. Having a car was essential to a salesman; he was happy to take on the debt with his new earning capacity.

Evidently E. F. had been listening carefully when Ed had discussed buying a car: his first choice was the 1949 Chevy. And he had wanted one with two doors. Ed had already begun his habit of thinking ahead. He knew the car he bought would still be with him when he married and had children. The thought of the children being able to open the back doors and fall out was frightening to him. The car in the driveway sported only two doors. Shortly thereafter, Ed filled up his car with gas—at 15 cents a gallon—and left for Fort Worth.

His time at Swift taught Ed much more than he, or his dad, ever expected. They assumed that Ed would gain experience in sales at a large ice cream company and eventually return to Blue Bell with enhanced knowledge and helpful suggestions for improving his dad's business. Instead, Ed learned much about how *not* to run a company.

In Fort Worth, Swift had two other salesmen, both of whom had remained with the company during World War II because they were classified as 4-F. After working with these two men and receiving hostile treatment from them, Ed wondered if their Selected Service classification reflected psychological problems rather than physical challenges. For example, when he first joined the company, the men refused to teach him anything about the business for fear that he would achieve more than they. They had no desire to work hard to get ahead at Swift or to promote the company, and instead they focused on keeping Ed from advancing.

When Ed landed a new drugstore account in Arlington, Texas, the Swift territory supervisor Bill Hosea was amazed. Why hadn't the other two salesmen acquired the long-standing business? Ed explained that they would have had to make an effort to acquire new accounts. Business was not going to walk through the office door on its own. Next, Ed had to convince the storeowner that Swift Ice Cream would enhance his fountain service and that he would be an excellent and attentive representative for the company. Ed even offered to teach the employees how to operate behind the counter, make popular ice cream concoctions, and figure out the costs to the drugstore so they would know how much to charge their customers. Ed's success reflected initiative, persuasion, and faithful adherence to his promises. The other salesmen were not willing to work that hard.

Ed's initial impact was so strong that, when the branch manager in Corsicana was fired because of a drunk driving accident in early 1950, Ed was chosen to take his place until an experienced manager could be transferred to Corsicana. While there, Ed managed the three ice cream delivery routes that operated out of the office. It was invaluable experience.

When the new branch manager arrived, Ed returned to the Fort Worth office, where his sales territory included half of Fort Worth and several communities to the west—among them Stephenville, Glen Rose, Meridian, Alvarado, and Itasca. Much to the chagrin of his associates, Ed excelled at developing new accounts for Swift. He added more business for the company than the other two "experienced" salesmen combined.

Meanwhile, he also gained management knowledge. At Swift there was no cooperation or coordination between sales and manufacturing, which interrupted smooth operating conditions. Therefore Ed decided that if he were ever in charge, those two aspects of the business would be thoroughly integrated—along with every other sector of the company.

He also realized that having everyone looking out only for himself was a prescription for a company's failure. Instead of promoting one's self-interest at the expense of others, Ed saw that teamwork was the best way to go. Not only would he provide plenty of opportunities for advancement, but each new employee would learn all about his own job and the company itself. If he became manager, Ed's top goal would be to have everyone working in the same direction at the same time.

Not all of Ed's time or attention was devoted to business during his years with Swift. Ed had decided early on that he wanted to get married at age 21. When he graduated from Texas A&M, he had achieved that age but realized he was still too young for marriage. Besides, he had no prospective wife in mind. He decided that he might be ready at 22.

Ed had definite ideas about what his future mate would be like. She would be pretty. She would belong to a Protestant faith, preferably

Lutheran. Her background would be rural in nature, and she would be able to work well with her hands. Ideally, she would have strong, straight teeth (since the Kruses' teeth tended to be crooked).

Ed had actually begun looking for a future wife during his freshman year at Texas A&M, figuring they could date for three years and marry when he graduated. Attending an all-male school and unable to afford much dating did not help matters, but his eyes and ears were open, and his scouts were out.

When he was a junior in college, Ed heard about two beautiful Blinn College freshmen who might be worth getting to know. Both of them were named Evelyn. Shy Ed failed to act. In the spring of his senior year at A&M, he asked his sisters Bertha and Mildred if they knew of someone he could ask for a date. Coincidentally, they suggested that he approach one of the Evelyns he had heard about the year before. Evelyn Delores Tiaden was from the Stone community near Brenham. Although she was two years behind him in school, Ed and Evelyn had actually been in confirmation class together at St. Paul's Evangelical Lutheran Church. Ed's only memory of her was that she was skinny, small, and "all knees."

Performing due diligence, Ed did some checking on Evelyn and her family to confirm that they were honorable people. Ewald Tiaden was a respected farmer who sold his produce in Brenham, and his wife Hildegard Sophie (Steinbach) Tiaden was active in the Ladies Aid at St. Paul's Evangelical Lutheran Church, even serving as president of the organization. Hildegard was the sister of Dr. Herbert L. Steinbach, a well-known ENT specialist in Brenham. Evelyn's brother John also passed scrutiny. Ed's investigation was not for snob appeal: he just wanted to avoid obvious scoundrels, like "town drunks."

With stellar information in hand, Ed asked Evelyn out on a date. By this time, Evelyn was completing her work at Blinn College. She accepted his invitation, and Ed prepared to do all the talking, because he had heard that Evelyn was a bit quiet. To his delight, the two of them were very comfortable with each other and found plenty to discuss. Ed liked Evelyn very much. After their third date, Ed told his friend Robert Gaskamp, "I'm going to marry that girl! *Period.*"

Evelyn's thoughts must have been along the same line. She was scheduled to begin nursing school in Galveston in September 1949. It was a four-year course, and the understanding with her parents was that if she began the program, she was committed to finishing it. Evelyn decided to postpone her matriculation for one year and get a job as a clerk in a jewelry store in Brenham. That way, she could discern Ed's true intentions.

Meanwhile, Ed went off to Fort Worth to begin his job with Swift. He remained loyal to Evelyn. It was obvious that Ed and Evelyn made an excellent match. Their backgrounds were very similar, and each certainly exceeded the other's expectations for a lifetime partner. The couple delighted in being together and spending time with the many friends they had in common—at parties, picnics, dances, bridge games, and so on. Ed began to think seriously about asking Evelyn to marry him.

For Christmas 1949 he gave her a hope chest. She was elated but thought that there might be an engagement ring hidden inside. There was not. It took Ed several months of earning a paycheck before he could afford a ring. On March 25, 1950, Evelyn's twenty-first birthday, Ed formally asked Evelyn for her hand in marriage and presented her with an engagement ring. She happily accepted his proposal.

It was Ed's desire to marry in June of that year. Ewald, Evelyn's father, asked if the couple could wait until the harvest season was over in the fall. Ed insisted on the earlier date. The wedding was set for Sunday, June 18, 1950. Several parties were held in the couple's honor leading up to the event, including the rehearsal dinner, hosted by E. F. and Bertha Kruse.

The rites took place at St. Paul's Evangelical Lutheran Church in Brenham, with the Reverend Theo R. Streng officiating the candlelight ceremony. Evelyn "wore a gown of nylon tulle and imported Chantilly

Ed and Evelyn Kruse prepare to cut their wedding cake on June 18, 1950. Pictured from left to right are E. F. Kruse, Bertha Kruse, Ed Kruse, Evelyn Tiaden Kruse, Hildegard Tiaden, and Ewald Tiaden. Courtesy of Ed. F. and Evelyn Kruse

Ed's 1949 Chevrolet is covered with wedding greetings. Courtesy of Ed. F. and Evelyn Kruse

lace appliquéd with crystal beads which fell into a cathedral length train." Around her neck was a string of pearls, a gift from Ed.

Following the ceremony, the Tiadens hosted a reception at their farm. Keeping with the prevailing traditions of the community, they served tea-cakes, cookies, finger sandwiches, punch, and coffee to their many guests.

Evelyn, who wore a pink linen suit with navy blue accessories and an orchid corsage, and Ed left for their honeymoon with many old shoes and tin cans tied to the bumper of the 1949 Chevy and shoe-polish greetings painted on their car windows. When they arrived at the cattle guard separating the Tiaden property from Highway 290, Ed cut the cans off (thinking ahead, he had a pair of scissors in the car) and left them in the road to hamper any mischievous pursuers. The couple spent their first night of married life in a hotel in Sealy, Texas. The next day, they drove to Galveston Island for fun in the sun. They stayed two nights at the Galvez Hotel and left on Wednesday to head to Corsicana so that Ed could report to his temporary branch manager position on Thursday.

Even though the young Kruses lived briefly in an apartment in Corsi-cana, they didn't establish their first true homestead until Swift transferred Ed back to Fort Worth. Finding an apartment proved to be a daunting task. Every time a new apartment appeared in the newspaper, it was either out of their budget range or was snapped up before Ed and Evelyn could rent it. They decided to stalk the *Fort Worth Star-Telegram* to get new listings just as they came off the press. One night, the perfect apartment became available. The couple immediately called Mr. and Mrs. Sam Sobel, even though it was 8 p.m., and asked if they could drop by and look at the apartment. Surprised at the call—since the papers had not yet hit the streets, the Sobels agreed, and the Kruses went, looked, and put down a deposit right then and there. They would live in that apartment for about six months, until they moved back to Brenham in February 1951.

What caused the return to Brenham? Ed and Evelyn went home one weekend for a visit. Ed's mother Bertha knew that E. F. needed help at Blue Bell. Yet E. F.'s pride prevented him from admitting to Ed that he wanted his son to leave Swift and come back home. Ed, even though he was disillusioned with Swift and Co., was as stubborn as his father. He refused to ask his father for a job. Somehow Bertha managed to appeal to both egos by saying, "*I'm* asking you to come back!" E. F. then offered Ed a position as a route supervisor, and Ed accepted. The young Kruses packed up for the move to Brenham.

At the time, Ed still owed E. F. $700 on his 1949 Chevrolet. Evelyn offered to pay off the note with money she had earned from raising chickens before she married. She spent the remainder on a sewing machine, which she still uses today. The couple returned to Brenham—out of debt and expecting their first child.

Chapter Seven

Do not compromise your principles.

• EDISM #20 •

ED'S NEW DUTIES at Blue Bell as a route supervisor were very similar to those he had been performing for Swift in Fort Worth. His territory included the rural area north of Brenham. It stretched northward to Marlin and eastward to Huntsville and Conroe. Ed also serviced Navasota, just northeast of Brenham.

In his white panel truck, Ed traversed his route. One of his duties was to set up advertising at the various grocery stores. This gave him an opportunity to recommend new ice cream flavors as they became available. At his sales locations, Ed also installed freezer cabinets, which small rural grocers used for displaying ice cream. This service to the grocers had come about recently when Blue Bell and other manufacturers began selling ice cream in half-gallon cartons. Thanks to the development of Freon as a coolant, post–World War II refrigerator/freezers and deep freezers were popping up in homes across Texas. This meant the consumer could take home more ice cream and keep the cartons frozen until ready to use. Thus the grocers also needed a way to keep the larger containers frozen.

Freezer cabinets were the answer, but they were also temporarily the bane of the ice cream industry. In the 1950s, grocers normally sold only one brand of ice cream. It might be Blue Bell from Brenham, Lilly from Bryan, Purity from Galveston, Carnation from Houston, or the products of about 20 other companies who competed in various areas of Central Texas. One way a salesman could entice a grocer to sell his brand of frozen desserts was to offer him a sparkling new freezer cabinet. It might be larger, more modern, or more technologically advanced than his current machine. When the grocer accepted the new freezer, he basically agreed to sell that company's products. The successful salesman installed the new cabinet, filled it with his cheapest products (to offset the cost of the new machine), and abandoned the old machine outside the store. E. F. Kruse usually counteracted this practice with his loyal customers by lowering his ice cream prices, but Blue Bell lost money in the process.

One of Ed's tasks was to pick up any rejected freezer cabinets that needed to come back to Brenham for reuse. Sometimes his duties expanded to delivering ice cream to customers when a driver-salesman was sick or needed help. Occasionally, Ed had to collect money from his customers. Most of them paid for their ice cream when it was delivered, but every so often E. F. allowed short-term credit. When the credit customers were slow to pay, Ed was responsible for making sure they settled their debts in a timely manner.

Being a people person, Ed enjoyed any reason to contact his customers. He took pride in servicing his route efficiently and keeping promises made to the grocers. Ed also looked for new business outlets that would sell Blue Bell Ice Cream in the areas he served.

In those early months at Blue Bell, Ed discovered a troubling situation. Many of the company's competitors were selling "mellorine" and passing it off as ice cream. The product was inferior, but it could be sold to consumers at a great profit to the manufacturers. Companies sold the product under such names as Frosty Crème or Mello Crème. Whatever the name, it was a frozen dessert product made using Mrs. Tucker's shortening (or some

Blue Bell's automotive fleet in the mid-twentieth century. Courtesy of Blue Bell Creameries

other brand), at 18 cents per pound, instead of the expected butterfat, at $2 per pound.

E. F. Kruse refused to make a nondairy frozen dessert. He felt it was unethical to make a product disguised as ice cream. Besides, the vegetable substitutes and lard he had used to manufacture the inferior ice cream during World War II still left a "bad taste in his mouth." E. F.'s solution was to manufacture a cheaper form of ice cream and sell it at mellorine prices. This practice was causing Blue Bell's profits to fall.

The frozen dessert product made with shortening or vegetable oils posed an industry-wide concern. In 1951 Ed attended a Texas Dairy Institute meeting in Dallas with his dad. There the delegates voted to require that, beginning the following January, the label "mellorine" be affixed to frozen dessert products made with substitutes for butterfat. With this designation, the consumer would be aware that the product was not truly ice cream. The decision did not change E. F. Kruse's mind about manufacturing mellorine, but at least he felt the consumers would be informed that they were not purchasing the real deal.

The mellorine issue quickly faded when E. F. became ill in the fall of 1951. The Brenham doctors sent him to specialists in Houston to address the severe pains he was having in his side. Their diagnosis was stomach cancer that had spread to his appendix and duodenum, the nearest portion of the small intestine to the stomach. E. F. underwent surgery at Memorial Hospi-

tal in Houston in early October. The operation was deemed a success, but an infection developed. Even the miracle drug penicillin was unable to control the infection. E. F. Kruse died on October 21, 1951 at the age of 56.

E. F. Kruse's sudden death was a blow to his family, to Blue Bell, and to the Brenham community at large. E. F.'s obituary makes this point most clearly:

(1895–1951) Eddie F. Kruse, 56, life-long resident of Washington County and for many years a leader in business, civic, church and club activities, died at Memorial Hospital in Houston at 10:15 Sunday morning. He was apparently recovering from a major operation when complications appeared that resulted in his death.

E. F. Kruse. Courtesy of Blue Bell Creameries

Funeral services will be held at St. Paul's Lutheran Church at
3:30 Wednesday afternoon, with Rev. Theo R. Streng officiating
and Leon Simank and Wm. H. Buske in charge of arrangements.
Preceding the church rites a service for the family and relatives will
be held at the Kruse residence, 810 South Austin, at 2:30 Wednesday. Burial will be in the family plot at Prairie Lea Cemetery.

The First National Bank and the Blue Bell Creamery will
remain closed Wednesday afternoon, as a tribute to the memory
of Mr. Kruse.

Born and reared in the Rocky Hill community Mr. Kruse has
resided in Brenham since early manhood. He was educated at
Blinn College and the Southwest Texas State Teachers College
at San Marcos and, after finishing college, taught school for a
short time. When a young man he became associated with the
local creamery, which developed into the Blue Bell Creameries
of which he had been manager for 32 years. He was prominent
in the ice cream industry in Texas, being past president of the
Texas Ice Cream Manufacturers Association and a director of
the Dairy Products Institute of Texas.

He was first vice president of the First National Bank of
Brenham, member of the city commission, and a former chairman of the county board of education. A leader in church work,
he was president of the Brenham Area Lutheran Brotherhood
and had long been a member of St. Paul's Lutheran Church. He
was a director of the East Texas Chamber of Commerce, past
president of the Brenham Chamber of Commerce, a Rotarian,
and a member of the Travelers Protective Association.

A veteran of World War I, Mr. Kruse was a past division
commander of the American Legion, as well as past commander
and one of the organizers of the Buddy Wright Post. During
World War II he served as chairman of the Washington County
Draft board for seven years.

He was married January 22, 1920, to Miss Bertha Quebe, who
survives. He also leaves three daughters, Mrs. Garrett Spitzer and
Miss Evelyn Ann Kruse of Brenham, and Mrs. Charles Bridges
of Edwards, Calif.; two sons, Edward F. Kruse of Brenham
and Howard Kruse, a student at A and M College; three little
granddaughters and one grandson; two brothers, Fritz Kruse of
Brenham and Willie Kruse of McGregor; and three sisters, Mrs.
Fritz Quebe, Miss Ida Kruse, and Mrs. Robert Wernecke, all

of Brenham. The active pallbearers were chosen from members of the Lutheran Brotherhood: C. D. Dallmeyer, M. H. Ehlert, W. B. Eimann, H. C. Hafer, Almot Schlenker, Ben Schleider, L. E. Seidel and Adolph Wiede. Honorary pallbearers are directors of the Blue Bell Creameries, employees of Blue Bell Creameries, directors of the First National Bank, American Legion, Rotary Club, City Commissioners, members of the Lutheran Brotherhood and all friends of the family.

Looking back, Ed Kruse realized that his father had not felt well for a long time. He suspected that E. F.'s stomach problems and exhaustion prompted his mother's plea for Ed to return to Brenham and to Blue Bell. His father truly needed help. Ed speculated that his father was feeling ill as far back as his senior year in high school when he was not up to traveling to some of his son's out-of-town football games. Nevertheless, no one suspected how serious E. F.'s symptoms were or that he might be facing death.

Everything seemed to be in limbo after E. F. Kruse died. The family, the company, and the community went through the paces of living, working, and serving, but the grief was deep. Not only did Ed feel like he had to step up to be the man of his birth family, but he also had Evelyn and their three-month old daughter Karen to support.

The directors at Blue Bell made no move to replace E. F. as manager. The company just worked as best it could without top leadership for about a month. Finally, Ed approached Herbert C. Hohlt, the president of the Blue Bell board of directors, and asked if he could be considered for his father's position as manager. The response was immediate and affirmative. The job was his.

The board had already considered Ed to be the most qualified candidate for the position. After all, he had grown up in the company, knew all the personnel, and had experience in most areas of the business. His degree in dairy manufacturing from Texas A&M provided another asset, as did his tenure outside the company at Swift. Herbert Hohlt had waited to approach Ed with the job offer until the young man had had sufficient time to grieve and to assess his next move. Ed's taking the initiative to ask to be manager indicated that he was ready to accept the challenge.

Therefore, at age 23—the same age his father became manager of Blue Bell—Ed took over the reins of the company. Reverberating in Ed's mind were E. F.'s tales of second-generation children who ruined their fathers' successful businesses. He was determined not to be one of them. His first step was to figure out how to make up for the $25,000 Blue Bell loss due to the cabinet wars and E. F.'s policy of selling ice cream at the same price as other companies' mellorine. Ed's first full year in charge, 1952, promised to be a real challenge.

Chapter Eight

Integrity is not negotiable.

• EDISM #3 •

ED KRUSE OFTEN SAID that the two best decisions he ever made in his business life were to come back to work at Blue Bell and to step into his father's shoes as head of the company. Midway through 1952, his first full year as manager, he might have thought differently. The obstacles he faced were daunting.

Ed's foremost goal was to complete the year in the black. He felt up to the task as far as producing sales, making ice cream, and handling the bookkeeping, but he doubted his purchasing and hiring abilities. His pluses would have to outweigh his minuses.

One of his initial tasks was to address the mellorine problem. Although his father refused to produce a nondairy frozen dessert, Ed took a different tack. Now that it was legal to do so, Blue Bell would develop the best mellorine available and charge customers the lower prices they desired. Meanwhile, the quality of Blue Bell's finest brand of ice cream would be enhanced. Blue Bell Supreme would contain only prime ingredients—the best sweet cream, milk products, sweeteners, fruits, and nuts. The consumer could rely on its consistent quality and deliciousness in every carton—in every spoonful. Its price would be higher than regular ice cream and mellorine, but it would be well worth the extra money. In all instances, consumers would know exactly what they were purchasing and that they would be getting an outstanding product at an excellent value.

Making exceptional products proved to be the least of Ed's worries. In the personnel department, at least three other people at Blue Bell felt they deserved the managing position more than Ed. Elton B. "Andy" Anderson was the toughest challenger. He had been with Blue Bell since 1930 when

The Blue Bell Creameries board of directors when Ed Kruse was the young manager of the company. Standing are J. W. Barnhill and Will Kolwes. Sitting are F. C. Winkelmann, H. C. Hohlt, and Ed Kruse. Courtesy of Ed. F. and Evelyn Kruse

E. F. hired the 14-year-old to work 2 hours and 15 minutes each day, picking the stems off strawberries for strawberry ice cream. He earned 7½ cents per hour. Andy's dad had lost use of his arm in a cotton gin accident, so the family needed as much income as possible. Andy's hours, income, and responsibilities gradually increased over the years—he had participated in most parts of both manufacturing and sales. When E. F. died, Andy was a route supervisor who covered half of Blue Bell's sales territory. Ed had serviced the other half before he succeeded his father as manager of the company.

After E. F.'s death, Andy came to Ed and told him that shortly before his dad went into the hospital he had promised Andy a handsome raise to keep Andy from going to work for Lilly Ice Cream in Bryan, Texas. Ed knew how valuable Andy was to the company, but he refused the raise. He told Andy that he had only Andy's word about the raise and that the company could not afford it. Andy stayed but was unhappy.

Ed then brought Vastine Pietsch in from La Grange to be route supervisor and to cover the half of Blue Bell's territory that Ed himself had serviced. Vastine had begun in the sales department in 1940, and, while living in La Grange, he delivered ice cream to Muellersville, Industry,

Frelsburg, Fayetteville, La Grange, and Hallettsville. Unfortunately, Andy tried to dissuade Vastine from moving to Brenham, but Vastine jumped at the opportunity for promotion. Ed not only needed the entire territory covered, but he also had to have an experienced salesman ready if Andy did, indeed, bolt to Lilly.

It pleased Ed to be able to work with Vastine on making effective sales calls. He traveled with his new salesman to small stores in rural areas. One of the calls was at Reuben's Grocery in Weimar. Ed wanted to help Vastine win the account from Carnation. To convince the owner of Blue Bell's strengths, Ed placed many of the company's ice cream cartons on the counter. He demonstrated to the owner that a company had to sell a lot of ice cream to produce so many flavors. The owner decided that Ed was right and changed his account to Blue Bell. Next, Ed and Vastine used the same approach at a store in Columbus. Vastine learned a great deal from Ed about how to get new business for Blue Bell and how to manage the accounts effectively. Ed encouraged and taught his employees, unlike the approach he had faced at Swift.

Disgruntled by Ed's attention toward Vastine, Andy Anderson's new ploy became to complain to all the customers along his route about everything at Blue Bell. Ed was ready to fire him. Finally, one of the grocers suggested that Andy either stop grousing and go along with the Blue Bell program or quit.

Suddenly, Andy had an epiphany. He walked into Ed's office and confessed, "Ed, I want to tell you something. I've done you wrong. I haven't been working. I haven't been doing my job. I want to tell you that I've got my head screwed on right now. I'm going to do a good job for you. Besides that, I think you were getting ready to fire me." Ed admitted that Andy was correct about everything he'd said. After their talk, Andy kept his word and returned to being a significant Blue Bell team member.

As it turned out, Ed *did* have to fire two employees early in his tenure. In fact, they were the only two people Ed ever dismissed during his active management at Blue Bell. Both were blatantly stealing from the company.

One driver salesman, who Ed initially pegged as a great guy, stole from Blue Bell by changing his load sheets: He would sell ice cream, but the invoice would show that he had sold a lot less. The salesman was keeping the cash difference. When Ed caught him, he had no choice but to let him go.

The other culprit was even more devious. His criminal act was to stay late during each lunch hour and sell four 4-gallon cans of ice cream to a friend. The invoice would show a sale for one 4-gallon can. The crony then took the ill-gotten goods back to his place of business and made quite a bit of money dishing out large scoops and double-dips of ice cream for a nickel. Later in the afternoon, the Blue Bell employee would meet his partner-in-crime and receive his cut of the action.

Ed caught on to the scheme one day when he was late leaving for lunch because he needed to fill his car with gas. He heard someone say, "Hold up. Don't do it. The boss is here." Ed observed four 4-gallon cans being put into a customer's car and asked to see the invoice. It noted sales of one 4-gallon can. Ed fired the thief on the spot, even though he swore that he had made a mistake on that day only. Ed cited that the man worked this spot every day and knew exactly what he was doing. Ed was no fool, and he couldn't abide someone who stole.

The firings made an impact. Ed had not intended to set an example, but the employees got the point. One of them exclaimed, "Ed ain't gonna put up with a bunch of foolishness."

At this juncture in his brief career as manager, Ed felt that he might finally be getting all the employees headed in the same direction—a lesson he had learned from the personnel problems at Swift. His actions about maintaining integrity within the company caused everyone to take notice.

Now he had to teach the vendors who tried to take advantage of Ed's youth and inexperience. E. F. Kruse had worked out a 2 percent discount and a 30-day period in which to pay bills with three of Blue Bell's largest vendors. Shortly after Ed took over, one of the vendors revoked the discount. Then a second followed suit. When the third supplier began discussing rescinding the discount, Ed challenged him with a look of defiance, and the vendor changed his mind. At that point, Ed quit doing business with the other two companies. Even though they came back to him and offered to reinstate the 2 percent discount, Ed would not relent. Those two suppliers had completely lost their integrity when they reneged on the agreement they had made with his father. Ed didn't do business that way, and he would not work with companies that did. Ed was probably not the only person who learned from that experience.

If Ed didn't already have enough on his plate, he still needed to deal with about twenty-five competitors whose territories abutted Blue Bell's, including Lilly Ice Cream in Bryan; Velvet in Corsicana; Anderson's in Temple; Superior Dairies, Borden's, Austin Made, and Lily Fresh in Austin; Borden's, Carnation, Sanitary, Sun Up, and Swift in Houston; Model Dairy, Purity, and Star Dairy in Galveston; and several more in other small towns. If each company spread out its territory for 60 or so miles like Blue Bell did, they were competing fiercely at their extremities.

Most ice cream tasted the same back then, so customers and consumers looked at price rather than quality. A 5-cent difference in a half-gallon carton could swing sales one way or the other very quickly. Some ice cream companies switched to flimsy rectangular half-gallon cartons to save money and pass the savings to the consumer. Grocers could be swayed to push a company's products or sell them exclusively if given discounts, freezer cabinets, neon signs, or even the promise of asphalting their parking lot. In other words, the ice cream companies attempted to "buy" their customers.

This form of competition was exasperating to Ed and many other managers. There was even an attempt to enact a law to prohibit the practice of "bribing" customers. Ed fought against that idea because he believed in a free market economy. Finally, his solution was simply to enhance substantially the quality of Blue Bell's products, price them accordingly, and provide the customers and consumers with the best service and value possible. No gimmies. No preferential discounts. The price list for all the grocers that Blue Bell sold to was the same. *Period*. Ed's philosophy proved to be a winning one.

During that first year of managing Blue Bell, Ed's hours were from 7:30 a.m. to 6:00 p.m. six days a week. He also came into the office for two hours on Sunday mornings to receive fresh cream from local farmers. He scheduled no vacation. He had his hand in every aspect of the company—paying bills by writing checks in longhand and posting the amounts to the correct accounts; improving formulas for ice cream; hiring and training personnel; purchasing ingredients, equipment, and supplies; developing a monthly profit and loss sheet; maintaining his commercial driver's license in case he had to substitute on routes; creating ads; and constantly watching the bottom line.

Fortunately, Ed did have some invaluable help. Edna Ruppert, formerly E. F.'s secretary, remained with Blue Bell and acted as a mentor to Ed after his father's death. She patiently taught him much about the administrative and accounting side of the business. Edna never married; her fiancé had been killed in World War I. She was totally devoted to the Kruses and to Blue Bell. Ed truly appreciated her excellence and loyalty.

Upon Miss Edna's semi-retirement in 1959, Ed commended her service to Blue Bell. He particularly praised the fact that she always had "an open mind to new ideas and concepts." The two of them did not agree on everything, but her attitude was a progressive "How can we do the job better?" or "I think we ought to change and do it this way," or "Yes, I think that would be a good idea." The employees listening to Ed's speech surely heard the emphasis he and Miss Edna placed on positive attitude and enthusiasm.

Reinhardt (R. H.) Loesch, the very capable plant superintendent, had been with the company since 1921. R. H. had little formal education, but he grew up in the plant and knew everything about it. Without Mr. Loesch to run the manufacturing processes, Ed's first year would have been even more difficult. Many other employees rose to the occasion and functioned beautifully under the new management.

Ed even brought in excellent hires of his own in those early days. For example, he had a tough time filling spots in the plant. After all, World War II had ended, and workers were needed everywhere to rebuild industries neglected during the war. Consumers eagerly bought cars, refrigerator/freezers, washing machines, new houses, and many other commodities. The demand for qualified workers was high.

It occurred to Ed that there was no reason why women couldn't work in the plant at Blue Bell. They certainly had proven their mettle and capabilities in manufacturing airplanes, tanks, and trucks during World War II. Therefore he placed an ad in the *Brenham Banner-Press* and invited women to apply for the openings. Ed hired the first six women he interviewed. They all had adult children and displayed the conscientious work ethic the positions required. Ed admited that when Reinhardt Loesch led the women into the plant that first day, the existing employees took a surprised glance. Other than that, the transition went smoothly. Ed delighted in the results of his innovative decision, and Blue Bell benefitted greatly.

Along with these successes, the young manager had early confirmation that he was doing something right when he received the following letter after only a few months on the job. Dated February 28, 1952, a representative of one of Blue Bell's flavoring suppliers praised Ed's efficiency and attention to detail:

Dear Mr. Kruse:

Recently, I checked your ledger sheet and felt that I should comment personally upon the excellent payment record you have established with us even though you probably regard it as a matter of course. You have made my job easier and more pleasant and whenever anyone has queried us for information concerning your company, it has been our pleasure to quote that fine record of yours and tell them how highly we regard you,

With best wishes, we are

Sincerely, A. E. Illes Company

George M. Illes

Another bold move Ed made early in his career as manager of Blue Bell was to begin closing the Lotta Cream "stores." The first location to go was in La Grange in 1952. The dip stations had been a boon to business during the Depression and World War II, when a double-dip cone for 5 cents was one of the few treats people could afford. However, the postwar boom had changed the dynamics. People no longer needed to eat ice cream while they were out and about. It was now possible to buy pints, quarts, and half-gallons to take home, store in their freezers, and dive into whenever the craving for Blue Bell Ice Cream struck. Had the Lotta Creams been actual ice cream parlors where consumers could sit and visit while they ate or where interesting ice cream concoctions could be created, Ed might have reconsidered his decision. The fact was the stores sold very small amounts of ice cream, created little profit, and didn't particularly enhance the image of Blue Bell. The home market became Ed's focus. *Period*.

With all the difficulties and changes Ed faced during his first full year as manager of Blue Bell Creameries, December 31, 1952, arrived quickly. To his delight, when he crunched the numbers, Blue Bell was in the black. The relief that washed over 24-year-old Ed Kruse caused him to break down in tears of joy. He had lived up to the commitment to his family. He had kept the company profitable for all the employees and their families. He had proven to his late father that this son would not be one who bankrupted his father's successful business. Most important, he realized that he loved his job and was becoming good at it. All of these facts bode well for the future of Blue Bell Creameries.

Chapter Nine

Keep things in perspective.

• EDISM #14 •

WHEN ED KRUSE BEGAN his tenure as manager at Blue Bell Creameries in 1951, the company employed thirty-five people, eight of whom worked chiefly with butter or received cream at the plant or at various stations in the Central Texas area. At that point, the company featured eight wholesale ice cream sales routes. The only ice cream plant was the original location in Brenham. Sales were confined to Central Texas and totaled about $250,000 annually. The company owned twelve vehicles. The growth over the next several decades would be remarkable.

In his first few years at the helm, Ed made many important improvements, changes, and decisions, but his main focus was to keep Blue Bell functioning well until his brother Howard could join him at the company. Ed felt that the synergy created by the two of them would not only keep their father's successful business growing but, at some point, they might also realize E. F. Kruse's fondest desire—to cover the state of Texas with their ice cream sales.

Howard William Kruse, two years younger than Ed, followed in his brother's footsteps and graduated from Texas A&M with a bachelor of science degree in dairy manufacturing. An outstanding student, Howard achieved the highest grade point average in the history of that program. Upon graduation in 1952, Howard accepted his commission in the US Army and served as a second lieutenant in Korea at the 38th Parallel. Having satisfied his two-year commitment, he reported to duty at Blue Bell Creameries in May 1954.

Ed attested that Howard was the best hire he ever made. That is saying a lot. Ed did not give himself much credit for Blue Bell's success, but he did feel that he was a good judge of potential excellence and that he helped assemble the outstanding team which moved the company forward.

It all began with Howard, who was not only intelligent but also attended greatly to detail. He was a perfectionist who was never happy until the result completely matched the goal. In addition, Howard excelled at watching the bottom line.

Ed cited several examples to demonstrate Howard's assets. For example, Charles Moser, publisher of the *Brenham Banner-Press*, once said about Howard, "Ask him what time it is, and he'll tell you how to make a watch." Ed would agree with the statement because it demonstrated Howard's meticulousness, as well as his understanding of machinery, not

Howard W. Kruse joined Blue Bell on a permanent basis in 1954. He took over the production side of the business and created many signature flavors, including Homemade Vanilla. Courtesy of Blue Bell Creameries

just his ability to utilize it. Running the plant required complete comprehension of mechanics, processes, formulas, and materials—plus the aptitude to integrate them effectively and efficiently. Ed asserted that no one in the United States could match Howard when it came to running an ice cream plant or knowing the intricacies of his product.

Ed also proudly proclaimed that Howard earned the reputation of being "the most demandingest man in Washington County." He ran a tight ship, but it paid off for Blue Bell. Howard's determination to maintain spotless machinery, to keep the floors in the plant dry (a real feat for an ice cream manufacturer), to purchase only premium and absolutely fresh ingredients at the best prices, to perfect flavors to their utmost deliciousness, and so much more enhanced the company.

Ed believed that Howard would deliver each carton of Blue Bell Ice Cream to every consumer's home freezer compartment if it were humanly possible to do so—that's how devoted Howard was to keeping his products at the ideal temperature and condition.

Ed also remarked, with a smile, that he's fortunate to be the older brother. He would have had a difficult time working under the exacting Howard.

Furthermore, Ed claimed that Howard still had the money the two made from working at Blue Bell when they were youngsters. This example emphasizes Howard's insistence that money be spent only when necessary. He always looked at expenditures from several different perspectives to discern not only the most effective but also the most economical approach.

Ed recalled fondly that when the two young men were students at Texas A&M and their father would give them each $5 when they were home on weekends, Ed went through his pretty quickly. Howard, on the other hand, always offered to share some of his with his big brother. Howard said he didn't really need it for anything, and besides it was all family money. Howard definitely had a generous side and was totally devoted to family.

When Howard came to work at Blue Bell, Ed was very much aware of Howard's attributes. Therefore, Howard was to focus on production and purchasing. His task was to improve every single product Blue Bell made and to buy the specific ingredients and supplies he needed to achieve that goal—all at the best prices. Ed also instructed Howard to run the plant in the most efficient manner possible. The ultimate goal was to provide the consumer the very best product at the very best value.

With Howard overseeing the plant, Ed himself could concentrate on his own strengths—sales, finance, and administration. Having established the division of duties, Ed served as general manager and secretary/treasurer of the company, and Howard took the title of assistant general manager.

Critics remarked that the Kruse brothers would never be successful at running their father's company because they were as different as chocolate and vanilla. Like this ice cream cone, their variant flavors served to complement each other. Courtesy of Blue Bell Creameries

Together, Ed and Howard monitored important changes and events during the latter part of the 1950s. They accomplished this despite their obvious youth and the carping critics who claimed that the two brothers—as different as vanilla and chocolate—could never succeed.

Ed and Howard proved them wrong by concentrating on their own areas of expertise and working out any differences before presenting a united front to the company and the public. Having been brought up in Blue Bell under the expert tutelage of E. F. Kruse and possessing the same strong values and goals, Ed and Howard knew that any disagreements between them were matters of varying approaches and of little consequence.

By consensus, the brothers continued Ed's practice of closing Lotta Cream stores in surrounding areas. They also shut down Blue Bell's adjunct butter plant in Giddings, Texas, in 1956 to consolidate that part of the business in Brenham.

In 1955 they had hired Kervin Finke to assist R. H. Loesch in superintending plant operations. Loesch was getting older so it seemed prudent to train someone eventually to take his place. Growing up in Prairie Hill and joining Blue Bell only a few days after his high school graduation, Kervin worked his way through the ranks. At each step he gained valuable experience through his quick grasp of the manufacturing procedures, his problem-solving abilities, and his strong work ethic. Kervin also displayed exceptional people skills. When it came time for R. H. Loesch to step down, Kervin was well prepared to take his place.

Even after Kervin became superintendent, R. H. continued to be employed at Blue Bell. In his 70s, R. H. still worked half a day and resented the fact that Kervin no longer allowed him to climb on top of the roof or the water tower to make inspections and repairs. Kervin himself retired in 2005 after 50 years at Blue Bell. R. H. Loesch and Kervin Finke are representative of the dedicated employees who have blessed this company.

In 1957 Blue Bell observed its fiftieth anniversary with an open house. Visitors watched the manufacturing process and received free cups of ice cream. Blue Bell also raffled off a deep-freeze unit to a lucky winner.

A year later, the brothers ceased butter manufacturing altogether. Although Blue Bell began as a butter company, sales had dwindled with the advent of oleomargarine following World War II. Oleo cost less, and homemakers, including Evelyn Kruse, preferred the butter substitute for sautéing since it heated to a higher temperature without burning.

Although some discriminating tastes still preferred sweet cream butter, the Kruses decided to focus exclusively on their ice cream sales, which were then approaching $1 million annually. Not only did that decision allow them to save the quality butterfat for their Blue Bell Supreme Ice Cream, but it also cut time from the work week. Ed no longer was required to spend two hours receiving fresh cream from farmers each Sunday morning.

Ed did not leave the local farmers without an outlet for their cream sales, however. While closing the cream station at the plant, he sold the other Brenham facility to Swift, which continued to buy cream and manufacture butter. Those steps satisfied everyone involved—Blue Bell, Swift,

Blue Bell Creameries celebrated its fiftieth anniversary in 1957. Courtesy of Blue Bell Creameries

farmers in the surrounding community, and the townspeople who preferred butter to oleo.

In the 1950s, the Kruses worked diligently to increase sales. Howard enhanced familiar flavors of ice cream and created new ones. An innovative carton hit the freezer cases. Instead of bluebell flowers adorning the packaging, the new carton's top featured a bell-shaped, see-through cellophane window so that consumers could view the delicious product inside.

New sales outlets came into focus, such as military compounds, prisons, and schools. Blue Bell even created specific treats for special events, like weddings, birthday parties, bridge games, and church socials.

The energy created by Ed and Howard was palpable. They quickly gained the confidence of Blue Bell employees. Even those with more years of experience put their dedication, work ethic, and enthusiasm behind the two young men's innovations.

Ed felt that a move he made in 1958 encouraged Blue Bell employees further. Having been at Swift—where everyone looked out only for themselves and not for the well-being of the company or other employees—Ed presented the board of directors with a plan. He wanted to make it possible for Blue Bell employees to buy stock in the company. With their hearts, minds, and pocketbooks invested in Blue Bell, Ed knew the loyalty would be there too.

The directors agreed and increased the number of shares in the company. Ed wanted to sell the shares at 70 percent of their value. Knowing that none of the employees could come up with cash to buy their allotment—one person was allowed to buy as much as $5,000 worth of stock— he asked Mr. Almot Schlenker at the First National Bank of Brenham for a special credit consideration. At the time the bank loaned money at a rate of 5 percent interest, but Ed requested that the Blue Bell employees be charged only 4.8 percent interest for their five-year term. Ed wanted to assure that the investors received a bit of the 5 percent dividend that Blue Bell was offering yearly, even while they were paying off their loans. Ed also guaranteed that Blue Bell would buy back stock if an investor defaulted and repay the loan with interest.

Mr. Schlenker told Ed that the bank never loaned money at a rate less than 5 percent. Ed responded that he sure wished Mr. Schlenker would present the proposal to the loan and discount committee. He added a veiled threat—he'd like to keep Blue Bell's accounts at First National Bank. Two days later, Ed had the deal and was able to offer the stock and loans to the employees.

Some of them questioned Ed's motives. Why would Ed want employees to have the stock if it were such a good deal? Why should they invest their hard-earned cash in Blue Bell shares? Suspicion abounded; many were unconvinced. The simple matter was that Ed thought commitment to the company would benefit everyone involved. And he was correct. Each of the fifteen employees who took the opportunity to invest at least $2,500 saw his stock grow to over $1 million in the ensuing years. In addition, by putting their own money in the pot, the employees were motivated to perform their best. Ed had everyone on the same team and headed in the right direction.

Those who didn't buy any stock at all or who didn't buy the maximum offered in 1958 later regretted it. Ed had a favorite story to describe the situation:

> In olden times, a man was riding his horse. It was dark, and he came across
> this creek and it was dry. When he got in the middle of the creek bed,
> a voice called out, "Stop!" Which he did, and he was mystified. It said,
> "Get off your horse." And, he did. "Now pick up some of the gravel from
> the creek bed and put it in your pocket." And, he did. "Now get back on
> your horse. Tomorrow morning you will be both glad and sad." The next

morning the rider looked in his pocket and he had rare jewels—diamonds and emeralds and pearls. And he was both glad and sad. He was glad that he had taken some and sad that he hadn't taken more.

The speaker Ed heard the story from was the president of a college in California, and he applied it to education. Ed felt that the story suited this case too. Those who bought just a little stock were glad that they had done so but sorry they had not purchased more.

Ed saw that Blue Bell continued to find ways for employees to acquire ownership in the company and to have excellent benefits. His team approach worked, and Blue Bell has some of the most qualified, dedicated, hard-working, long-standing employees anywhere. Their contributions to the company are directly responsible for the growth and success of Blue Bell Creameries.

Offering stock to employees is one of the few contributions Ed Kruse took some credit for toward the success of the company. What tickled him most was that those who invested their hard-earned dollars ended up with quite a nest egg with which to retire. It was a win/win situation for all.

While Ed managed Blue Bell in the 1950s, Evelyn was busy at home. When the couple first moved back to Brenham in 1951, Evelyn was pregnant with Karen, who arrived on July 3 that year. Ken was born on May 12, 1953; Paul, on October 7, 1954; and Neil, on April 7, 1958. During 10 years of washing cloth diapers and keeping up with four active little people, Evelyn orchestrated three moves for the family.

Ed and Evelyn first lived in the house on West Fourth Street, where Ed had been born. They rented the top east-side apartment. Shortly thereafter they relocated to another rental situation at 201 East Stone Street. Finally, they bought a former rental property from the Gross family. Located at the corner of South Park and Germania Streets, they moved into it in 1957 and lived there for the next 10 years.

Their plan sounds simple until we note the extensive remodeling needed. The Kruses lowered the house, redid the plumbing and electricity, and added a room and a garage. They did hire one carpenter to build the kitchen cabinets and place Formica on the counters, but the rest of the work was "do it yourself." Evelyn's dad—Ewald Tiaden—helped Ed with some of the construction and with painting walls and cabinets, laying tile, and wallpapering. Evelyn's mother Hildegard, Ed's mother Bertha, and Ed's sister Evelyn Ann stepped in to babysit when needed.

The result of their labors was an ample, one-story home for the young family of six. It featured three bedrooms—one for Ed and Evelyn, one for

Karen, and one for the boys—and two bathrooms, one ostensibly for the parents and the other for the children. There was a desk for each child— and one brand-new set of the *World Book Encyclopedia* to assist their studying. In the family room, the main focus was the Kruses' first television set. Just as Ed's birth family had sat around the radio listening to favorite shows, the next generation spent some of their family time watching television staples of the 1950s, like *Howdy Doody Time, Sky King, The Lone Ranger, Your Hit Parade*, and *I Love Lucy*. Ed's favorite was *The Bob Hope Show*.

Part of the house was centrally heated, but those rooms that were not had stoves for warmth when needed in the winter. The house was not centrally air-conditioned; window units kept the house cool during the hot Central Texas summers. In the yard were two notable trees, which helped shade the home—a pine in the front yard and a big pecan at the side. The children had plenty of room to run and play, and they could shoot basketballs at the hoop in the yard.

With his bustling family, a growing business, and a spacious home, Ed looked the picture of success. And he was. However, the constant stress was taking its toll. At one point Ed was getting so little sleep that Evelyn was worried that he was working himself to death. It wasn't just the problems at the office, the renovations to the house, and the efforts to spend time with their young children. Ed was also attending meetings all the time—at the church, in the community, and in the dairy industry. Finally, Evelyn insisted that he stop everything and go to bed for three days. He protested vociferously but followed her directions. She kept him in a dark room, fed him nutritious foods, intercepted all phone calls, and simply removed all pressures from his life. He emerged from the treatment realizing that she had been exactly right. He asked her to please repeat the process if he ever reached that dire state again. In the meantime, he strove to moderate his lifestyle.

No longer working on Sundays, he soon cut back the hours for weekdays. He and the rest of the employees arrived at 8:00 a.m. and left at 5:00 p.m. Soon Saturday hours were pruned too. Blue Bell chiefly used that day for manufacturing catch-up and machinery repair.

The shorter hours not only reflected Ed's determination to take better care of himself and his employees, but they also represented more efficient procedures at Blue Bell. The team was busier than ever. It readied for stiff competition as it looked 70 miles to the southeast and prepared to enter Houston's ice cream market.

Chapter Ten

Aptitude is important, but so is attitude.

• EDISM #7 •

WHY IN THE WORLD would Ed Kruse decide to take on the big ice cream companies in Houston, Texas? The answer is that there was simply nowhere else Blue Bell could grow. As 1960 arrived, the company's sales territory had already spread to the outskirts of Houston. In addition, population studies demonstrated a developing trend from rural to urban. It made no sense to expand farther into the less-populated areas of Texas: most of the people who would buy the ice cream were headed to Houston, San Antonio, Austin, and Dallas/Fort Worth.

Moreover, Ed felt the quality of Blue Bell's ice cream and frozen treats was superior to the products of Carnation, Swift, Borden, Sanitary, Foremost, and Sun Up. He also knew that his overall company plan was definitely better than Swift's—and maybe that of the other companies as well. But his true weapon lay in the team members he was beginning to assemble.

Ed was hesitant to single out employees, because each and every team member at Blue Bell was not only important but also essential to its growth, success, and reputation. However, he found it necessary to mention certain key players. They proved to be outstanding leaders and made exceptional contributions. In addition, their attributes provide a view into Ed's hiring strategy, which he considered to be one of his most important assets for Blue Bell.

In a football analogy, Ed Kruse would be head coach at this point in the history of Blue Bell. (Keep in mind that positions changed over the years.) He had already signed the head of the production side of his team—his brother Howard. Now he searched for a recruit to spearhead sales into Houston. His scouting reports helped him zero in on a potential phenom.

John W. Barnhill Jr. grew up in Brenham. The son of a local druggist, John worked at Blue Bell during the summers, like so many other local teenagers. John quickly demonstrated that production was not his area of expertise. Early in his career, he dropped a 10-gallon can of ice cream on his toe, breaking it. Searching for somewhere else to place a young man on crutches, Ed discovered that John was clever with words and could draw cartoons. Therefore, he used a Barnhill saying or two in ads and sent John to grocery stores to promote specials by sketching figures onto their plate-glass windows. For example, with the owner's permission, John might depict an exaggeratedly long dachshund on the window with the words, "Blue Bell Ice Cream is Doggone Good!"

Ed kept up with John's excellent academic performance in high school and his unusual leadership ability: John proposed and coordinated the

Ed took a big risk in setting his sights on Houston and competing with the large ice cream companies there. Courtesy of Blue Bell Creameries and Tracey Bryan

first class trip ever for Brenham High School seniors. Upon graduation, John attended the University of Texas at Austin and majored in journalism. He continued to work at Blue Bell during summers. One thing that impressed Ed was John's involvement in the student body at UT. John accepted the responsibility for organizing a huge social function on campus, and it went off without a hitch. At the same time, John was writing proclamations and speeches for George Christian, press secretary to Governor Price Daniel. Mild-mannered, always on an even keel, and pleasant to everyone he met, John managed to bring people on board and accomplish complex tasks.

John earned his journalism degree and accepted a position in Houston with the *Houston Press*. Ed maintained contact with John during this period and also while John served a six-month stint in the US Army Reserves. John aimed to become an eminent newspaper columnist in Houston and eventually own a small-town newspaper.

Ed Kruse proposed an alternative plan to John Barnhill. In 1960 he recruited the young man to join the Blue Bell team and lead the charge into Houston. Ed's instruction to his quarterback on this side of the business was simply, "Sell all the ice cream you can!"—at least that was the brief version. The complete game plan for securing a foothold in Houston was to target independent grocers and convenience stores and convince them that Blue Bell offered

1. Top quality products
2. Personal service
3. Sincerity and enthusiasm
4. Merchandizing and marketing aid to help move more product

Ed gave John a few of Ed's own business cards (John would have to scratch out Ed's name and insert his own), set him up in the trailer in Houston that would serve as Blue Bell's first "branch," and asked him to share a large metal desk and telephone with Marvin Giese, who was overseeing Blue Bell's small vending machine business in the Houston area.

Blue Bell had bought ninety-one vending machines and a small, refrigerated truck from Sun Up in October 1960 and later added machines from Snappy Snap Vending and South Texas Vendors. With Marvin in charge, Blue Bell had begun selling its ice cream treats in large downtown Houston office buildings and recreational facilities. Unlike prior vendors, Blue Bell found the business to be relatively profitable. The company's vending machines were located in a highly populated and condensed area of

Houston. Marvin Giese could fill the machines frequently and provide Houstonians an opportunity to sample Blue Bell frozen snacks.

With Marvin running the vending operation smoothly, it soon became clear that Ed Kruse had signed the right person to handle the rest of the Houston sales. Given the play, John ran with it. Not only did he service the thirteen accounts that Blue Bell already had on the outskirts of Houston, but he also developed new business—one small family grocery store at a time. John accomplished this by taking samples to the owners and persuading them to put Blue Bell Ice Cream into their freezer cases. The "moms and pops" were generally not too hard to convince once they tasted the products. Howard Kruse assured that Blue Bell Supreme Ice Cream lived up to its name in every way—top ingredients, taste, texture, and strict temperature control from the plant to the grocer's freezer case.

After office hours each day, John continued to give Houstonians opportunities to experience Blue Bell products. He sold samples from his three-wheel Cushman motor scooter in various neighborhoods. If people liked what they tasted, he encouraged them to ask that Blue Bell be put into their own grocers' freezers. At night, he telephoned Houston residents who had relatives in Brenham, told them where Blue Bell Ice Cream was available, and asked them to frequent those stores.

The first big break John had was when Sacco's, the most successful independent grocery store in Houston, agreed to sell Blue Bell Ice Cream. At that point, the larger ice cream companies became alarmed and spread the word that grocers shouldn't rely on Blue Bell. After all, its plant was located in a rural town in Central Texas and couldn't compete with the factories right there in Houston.

John Barnhill's ads countered that Blue Bell was better *because* it was made at the "little creamery in Brenham." The people in that German community were persnickety about quality and service and would send only the very best products to the ice cream lovers in Houston. John's ploy worked. Before the decade was over, Target, the newest discount chain store in Houston, accepted Blue Bell. Then Weingarten's, Houston's largest grocery store chain, came on board. Others followed.

The additional sales in Houston tested everyone's mettle. In those early days when one of the Houston grocery chains ran a special on Blue Bell, all Brenham hands, including Ed, pitched in to load trucks and do whatever else was necessary to provide the promised cartons of Blue Bell Ice Cream. Howard had the responsibility of keeping up with the production demand and ensuring the utmost quality.

As business increased, more excellent players were recruited, among

From the #1 Creamery in Brenham.

These young men, hired by Ed Kruse in the 1960s, would rise to leadership positions at Blue Bell. Pictured from left to right are Larry Ainsworth, Melvin Ziegenbein, John Barnhill, and Ray Schomburg. Courtesy of Blue Bell Creameries

them Larry Ainsworth, Melvin Ziegenbein, and James Liepke. All three of these young men spent part of their Blue Bell sales careers in Houston under John Barnhill's guidance and rose to commanding positions as Blue Bell grew. They came to the company from various parts of Texas—Houston, Burton, and Brenham, respectively—and with differing educational experiences, ranging from little college education to a mathematics degree from Texas A&M University. Ed saw something in these men that compelled him to have them on the squad. He looked for attitude along with aptitude and their understanding of what Blue Bell was all about. Ed treasured work ethic, character, loyalty, and enthusiasm, and he preferred to hire those who would become team players rather than stand-alone superstars. He recognized such qualities in these men and in so many other employees over the years.

Ed Kruse discussed his hiring practices in an article in *The Scoop*, Blue Bell's in-house newspaper, in November 1979:

> I am convinced that our people perform as they do because they have
> healthy attitudes toward themselves and their world. H. A. Westphall of
> the J. W. Newman Corporation has analyzed the attitudes of top workers

and concluded that several elements consistently characterize these people: a feeling of self-esteem; a sense of responsibility; communicativeness and the ability to relate to others; trust that others also try to do well; a spirit of joy in living and a sense of immediacy or "nowness"—the feeling that decisions should be made and action taken *now*, not because you are forced to take action, but because you *want* to. This analysis suggests that super performers are not always obsessive, humorless workaholics, but may instead be exceptionally nice people to be around. It's something for all of us to strive for—each of us, in our own way, in our own niche in life, can be a super performer.

In 1969 Ed and John added Lyle Metzdorf to the team. His role was more of assistant coach than player on the field. He and his business partner Clyde Burleson basically designed and managed every aspect of Blue Bell's advertising until Lyle's untimely, tragic death in 2002. Clyde continues to consult with Blue Bell to this day.

Born in Kansas in 1935, Lyle grew up in Independence, Missouri. He studied at the Kansas City Art Institute and School of Design before serving in the military, working for Hallmark Cards in Kansas City, and animating films in California. He eventually settled in Houston where he and Clyde formed the Metzdorf Agency in 1965. Lyle was one of several advertising experts whom Ed and John Barnhill considered hiring when it became evident that growing sales in the Houston area demanded John's full attention.

Ed had interesting comments concerning his initial contact with Lyle. When the other candidates arrived in Brenham for their interviews, they sat down with Ed and John and discussed how much the advertising budget should be and how to divide it between television, radio, and point-of-purchase accounts. Lyle, on the other hand, wanted to know more about the company, the products Blue Bell made, and what everyone did. He spent three days in Brenham—mainly watching what was going on in the plant. Then he talked with Ed and John about what approach he thought they should take toward advertising. Ed was impressed with the fact that he wanted to do a well-considered service for Blue Bell, not just peg the company into a budget with slots. Ed knew Blue Bell had found its creative genius.

As it turned out, Lyle Metzdorf continued in the same direction that John Barnhill had already taken the advertising. He focused on the benefits of eating ice cream from the "little creamery in Brenham." He himself loved the taste of Blue Bell Ice Cream and believed that if he could get

Ed Kruse made sure that Blue Bell Supreme Ice Cream contained only the very best ingredients. Courtesy of Blue Bell Creameries

a consumer to try the product just once, flavor would win them over and loyalty would follow. Tempting buyers with such phrases as "Blue Bell's the Best Ice Cream in the Country," "We Eat All We Can and Sell the Rest," "Blue Bell's Better by a Country Smile," "Have Yourself a Blue Bell Country Day," "Blue Bell Tastes Just Like the Good Old Days," and "The Cows think Brenham's Heaven," Lyle oversaw radio spots, television commercials, carton design, point-of-sale banners, and much more.

Ed Kruse added two important members to his administrative staff in the late 1960s, and they remain with the company today. Ruth Goeke came to Blue Bell in June 1967. Since there was no office position available, Howard interviewed Ruth and hired her to work in the plant. Ed had other plans for Ruth, however. She was a smart, talented young woman— Ed knew that because he purposely kept up with high-achieving Brenham High School students through articles and honor rolls posted in the *Brenham Banner-Press*. That same October, Bertha Kruse Spitzer, Ed and

Howard's oldest sister, who was their secretary and served as the company receptionist, decided to join her husband Garrett in a business venture. Ed knew exactly who he wanted to take Bertha's place at Blue Bell. He offered 18-year-old Ruth Goeke the job. Ruth expressed reluctance to accept the new post since she had made friends on the production line. Ed made a deal with her—come work in the office for two weeks. If she wanted to return to the plant, she could. Ruth agreed and never looked back.

Ed recounted that Ruth started out with a manual typewriter and a crank-handled adding machine. "Each time a word processor, a computer, or another new piece of technology has come along, she's balked a little— not sure whether she will like that or not. But she would try it and see," he reported. Ruth evolved with the company just as many other employees did. Growing up on a cotton farm, becoming administrative assistant to top management at Blue Bell Creameries, and even greeting and corresponding with US presidents was quite a ride for Ruth. Ed saw in that young high school graduate an eagerness to learn and achieve. He knew she could handle a new situation before she realized it herself. Incidentally, if readers ever need to know anything about Blue Bell or locate any document, they should ask Ruth. After 48 years with the company, she's currently the longest-serving employee, and she's forgotten nothing along the way.

In 1990 Ed entered Ruth Goeke in the *Brenham Banner-Press* contest to determine the "World's Greatest Secretary." Among many other compliments he gave Ruth in his nominating letter, Ed said, "She is intelligent, friendly, courteous, and has an extremely pleasant attitude day in and day out. She not only seems to enjoy her work, but she does a tremendous amount of it!" He also mentioned that her skills were versatile enough for her to be executive assistant to the president, the chief financial officer, and legal counsel for Blue Bell. Needless to say, Ruth Goeke won the title.

Diana Markwardt also applied for a position in 1967. She had graduated from high school in nearby Bellville, Texas, with an A+ average. Everything about Diana was perfect—her grammar, her spelling, her appearance, her handwriting, and her manners. Ed told her he would absolutely not hire her. Shocked, Diana asked, "Why?" Ed replied, "You've got high grades. You need to go to college, and I'm not going to stand in your way." Diana told Ed that she was burned out. Ed made a deal with her: if Diana attended college for one year and still wanted to work at Blue Bell, he would create a position for her. After a year at Blinn College, she returned and Ed hired her. She eventually became the vice-president in charge of office operations. Diana superbly manages all office personnel and functions, oversees each technological change that the company undertakes, and accepts every challenge given to her without batting an eyelash. Her accomplishments are performed so smoothly and efficiently that Ed says, "There is absolute peace in the family."

As exemplified by Ruth and Diana, Ed was a strong believer in hiring people who made top grades in school for administrative positions. He knew for a fact that they were accurate, they attended to details, and they were perfectionists. Plus they grasped new concepts quickly, they worked hard, and they didn't hesitate to undertake the toughest projects.

Ed was assembling an excellent team during the 1960s, and it's a good thing he did, because Houston wasn't the only challenging market Blue Bell would face.

Chapter Eleven

Work, don't worry.

• EDISM #30 •

WHILE JOHN BARNHILL led the consolidation of sales in Houston, which was 70 miles east of Brenham, an opportunity suddenly appeared in Austin, 90 miles west of Brenham. Chester Brooks, who owned Lily Fresh Ice Cream, called Ed Kruse in 1965 and asked him if Blue Bell wanted to buy his business.

Ed jumped at the chance. Blue Bell really had all it could handle at the moment, but Austin would have been the next logical direction if the company wanted to continue expanding. In this way, Ed set up Blue Bell's pattern of slowly growing into richly populated territories contiguous to those the company already served. He couldn't allow this opportunity to slip through his fingers.

The decision made, Ed knew he had only one person who qualified to manage the Austin branch—Clarence Jaster. Clarence had joined Blue Bell in 1948 at the age of 16 and had risen to become a sales supervisor in Brenham. Clarence absolutely did not want to go to Austin. Ed told him flat out that he was the only person in the company ready to handle such a responsibility and if he didn't agree to the promotion, Blue Bell would have to turn down the Lily Fresh offer. Seeing a hint of give on Clarence's part, Ed negotiated a deal: if Clarence ran the Austin branch for three years and still wanted to return to Brenham, Ed would consent. That arrangement would allow some of the newly hired sales team in Houston enough time and experience to be considered for branch management.

Just as Ed had helped Vastine Pietsch transform into a salesman, he was constantly available to Clarence as he grew into a branch manager. Many phone calls transpired between Austin and Brenham.

Superior Dairies provided the chief competition in Austin. Occasionally Clarence would call Ed and hint that Blue Bell should sell its ice cream cheaper in that market than in Houston. Ed would not relent: all customers everywhere Blue Bell was sold would receive the same pricing. *Period*. Ed suggested that Clarence push Blue Bell's mellorine products if price were an issue, but Clarence admitted that Austinites wanted ice cream. Ed remarked that ice cream cost more to make than mellorine, but Blue Bell's ice cream was a superior product and an excellent value. Austin residents would soon recognize that fact. Ed asked Clarence to have confidence in the program.

In another case, Clarence asked Ed to have Howard produce a milk chocolate ice cream in addition to its Dutch chocolate flavor. The folks in Austin seemed to prefer Superior Dairies' chocolate over Blue Bell's. Ed responded that the capital's citizens just hadn't had enough time to adjust their tastes to Blue Bell's first-rate chocolate: they were simply accustomed to the processed chocolate made in the United States. Ed convinced Clarence that Blue Bell had the best products in place. It simply would take time to educate Austinites. Clarence had to admit that Ed was right when Superior Dairies began making its own version of Dutch chocolate ice cream.

Ed had promised Clarence that he would hold his hand as he settled into his new position as branch manager. After several months of constant phone calls between Austin and Brenham, Ed was confident that Clarence was ready to make his own decisions. One day when Clarence called to complain about a relatively minor matter, Ed facetiously announced that the center ceiling of the plant had just collapsed and operations were virtually shut down. Clarence would have to handle the situation on his own. Clarence got the point and remarked, "Ed I don't have *any* problems!"

Although Clarence got the branch running very smoothly, he did not immediately adjust to living in Austin. Even as he approached his third year, he seemed eager to return to Brenham. But something happened. Perhaps he and his family made more friends and felt settled in the community. Maybe as ice cream sales increased, Clarence saw the results of his efforts and took pride in being Blue Bell's face in Austin. Possibly he relished the movement of the branch offices from the former Lily Fresh building, which Clarence constantly repaired on his own time, to the new Blue Bell facilities. Whatever transpired, Clarence volunteered to stay until his retirement in 1994. He developed an extremely successful Austin market.

As if the little creamery weren't busy enough keeping up with sales in the new Houston and Austin markets, Blue Bell began jobbing operations in 1967. In other words, the plant made popular nationwide products to sell

Blue Bell produced Baby Ruth Ice Cream Bars and sold them to other ice cream companies in Texas for distribution across the state. Courtesy of Blue Bell Creameries

to other ice cream companies, who would wholesale them to grocers, who would then retail them to consumers. The Baby Ruth Ice Cream Bar was the prime example. The Waukesha Fruit Company franchised the Baby Ruth Bar to Blue Bell. Given the recipe, Blue Bell made the well-liked treat and sold it to other ice cream companies across Texas. The Baby Ruth Bar could then be widely distributed to eager shoppers. Howard did such an excellent job of producing the Baby Ruth Bars that Blue Bell received franchises for other favorite items, like Popsicles, Drumsticks, Fudgsicles, Eskimo Pies, and Creamsicles.

Part of the reason the company met with success in this endeavor was because Howard installed the first Vitaline in the plant in 1965. This machine automated the processes of making frozen snacks. A Vitaline could make 600 dozen frozen snacks per hour and required much less manpower than the 500 dozen hand-produced items made per day previously.

Another new venture that Blue Bell tried in the late 1960s was opening two Sugar Plum stores in Houston. These ice cream parlors featured Blue Bell Ice Cream and also sold Lamme's Candies, which were made in Austin. Ed thought that the Sugar Plums would encourage ice cream consumption year round, not just in the summertime. He was correct to a point. Consumers wanted ice cream all the time, so the stores had to stay open for long hours every day of the week—requiring many employees to dip the ice cream and manage the sales. In the end, the Sugar Plum stores lost money ($5,329 in 1968), and Ed closed them within a year of their opening. Ed pointed out that he wanted Blue Bell employees to work fewer hours, but the Sugar Plum stores actually increased their time on the job. He remarked, "We learned our lesson. We are not in the retail business. We are strictly wholesale. *Period.*"

The Blue Bell plant hummed along during the summers of the 1960s with its ice cream and frozen snack production. In the slower winter months, the employees repaired and upgraded old machines, installed new equipment, and altered the building to make way for increased manufacturing operations.

For a few years, the company sold fireworks during the Christmas/New Year's holiday. This endeavor probably netted a little cash, but it reinforced to Ed that Blue Bell needed to "dance with who brung you" and concentrate on its ice cream and frozen snack sales.

As it turned out, Blue Bell's sales increased in the double digits percentage-wise each year during the 1960s—a remarkable record. After a few years in Houston and a report that showed Blue Bell owned ½ of 1 percent of the ice cream market share there, Ed began tracking that statistic for Blue Bell's various markets. The end of the decade showed that Blue Bell had an 18 percent market share in Houston—an impressive feat for the Little Creamery in Brenham.

Ed championed the determined underdog. One of the books he recommended to friends is *Twelve Mighty Orphans* by Jim Dent. It's the true story of a gifted and dedicated football coach, Rusty Russell, who took ragtag groups of orphans at the Fort Worth Masonic Home during the years of the Great Depression and formed football teams that competed successfully against teams from the finest high schools in the state of Texas. The Masonic Home had to scrape together used uniforms, pads, and equipment. The rundown bus Coach Russell drove to their games threatened to break down every time they drove it. They had one substitute at best. There were no loving, enthusiastic parents to cheer for them.

The odds these young men overcame each season seemed insurmountable, but year after year, they appeared in the state championship finals or semifinals. Their story is truly inspirational—a sterling example of the victories that raw talent, hard work, superb coaching, and sheer determination can bring.

Blue Bell, too, was up against incomprehensible odds in the 1960s. Would the company continue to make inroads and eventually compete on a more equal footing with the large ice cream manufacturers? That answer remained to be seen.

With Howard Kruse on the team, however, Blue Bell had a fighting chance. In the late 1960s, some of the salesmen challenged Howard to develop a vanilla ice cream that tasted just like the hand-cranked home-made versions they remembered from their childhoods. Howard spent about a year on the project, coming up with several attempts as he adjusted flavor and tex-ture. Finally, he thought he had reached the right combination. In December 1968 he submitted his sample to Ed, who agreed that the result was perfect. How-ard produced a batch of 500 car-

Blue Bell Homemade Vanilla, created by Howard Kruse, first appeared in stores in 1969 and quickly became the company's number-one flavor. It remains at the top of the chart today. Courtesy of Blue Bell Creameries

tons, and they were snapped up instantly. Blue Bell Homemade Vanilla Ice Cream has been the company's signature flavor ever since.

The 1960s were a banner decade for Howard Kruse in another import-ant way. He married Verlin Kautz, from Brenham, on November 11, 1962, and their four children were born almost exclusively in that decade: Diane (1964), Kathyrn (1965), David (1967), and Jim (1970). Life was busy and good for the Kruses.

Chapter Twelve

Maintain a sense of humor.

• EDISM #15 •

WHILE HOWARD'S FAMILY was just getting started, Ed and Evelyn had a houseful of teens and preteens. With school activities, sports, church youth groups, scouting, and more, the Kruse family was often going in many different directions at the same time.

Despite their hectic lives, Ed and Evelyn set high standards for their children and emphasized the benefits of hard work, being prepared, and planning ahead in achieving their goals. They were determined to pass down these principles to their offspring. Many teaching opportunities arose over the years.

For example, Karen once brought home an *F* in math on her fifth-grade report card. A smart girl, Karen had obviously not mastered the required concepts. Ed sat down with her every night for two weeks and taught her everything she needed to know about decimals and percents. After each study session, Karen would complete the twenty or so problems on her homework sheet. Then Ed would check her answers. When he handed the paper back to her, he might tell her that she had two wrong. To Karen's frustration, he never pointed out *which* answers were incorrect. In essence, Karen did the entire assignment again. She got plenty of practice during those two weeks and received an *A* on her next report card. Humbling for Karen and time-consuming for Ed, the extra effort was required on both their parts. Karen learned that some concepts take more work than others to master.

Another example is when Ed encouraged Paul to challenge himself by entering the chin-up contest in the countywide sports meet for elementary students. He installed a chin bar in the doorway of his sons' room and suggested that Paul practice every time he walked through. In the meet, Paul's classmate chinned twenty-two times and beat Paul's record of twenty-one. Paul didn't continue to practice for the following year's contest, because he figured the same boy would beat him again. Ironically, the boy moved from Brenham before the meet took place. The champion that year chinned only eighteen times. Paul would have won easily. He learned a valuable lesson about staying the course and being prepared.

Ed Kruse coached his sons and their fellow Boy Scouts in swimming, diving, and lifesaving. The boys participated in many meets over the years. At one competition, Neil, who had never lost a race, came up against a much taller, stronger scout. Ed helped Neil size up his opponent and suggested that his son take only three breaths as he swam the length of the pool—since raising his head to breathe tended to slow him down. Neil agreed and heeded his dad's advice. Although the larger boy took a three-foot lead, Neil caught up and won the race by a foot. Planning ahead certainly worked in this instance.

Ed and Evelyn must have felt successful in their parenting skills at this point. They were able to teach clear lessons through actual circumstances. However, there was one situation that absolutely befuddled them. The four Kruse kids were swimming in a creek on their Tiaden grandparents' farm. Nearby were some grapevines that they could use to swing over the water and drop in. At one point, Ken refused to relinquish his vine and thereby prevented his siblings from swinging into the pond. When Ken went inside, the others got their .22 rifle and shot the grapevine above where Ken had been holding it. The shot weakened the vine, and Ken fell into mud on his next swing. Ken was a mess, but all four Kruse kids got into trouble.

Ed had been very responsible in teaching his children how to use guns. He enjoyed shooting targets with them and taking them duck and dove hunting. Before each outing, Ed reviewed every safety lesson with the kids—how to carry the gun properly, how to hold it when climbing over a fence, where to aim to keep everyone else safe, when to release the safety catch, and so on. Ed never thought that he would have to emphasize, "Don't endanger your brother!" *He* learned a lesson this time: don't assume!

Keeping up with the four children was a challenge for Evelyn. She now remarks that if she had a nickel for every time she asked, "Where's Neil?" she would be a wealthy woman. The youngest Kruse kid did his very best to tag along with his siblings.

What Ed most liked to remember about those years were the vacations when the entire family spent time together. There were no competing activities, and everyone was in the same place at the same time. Ed modeled his father in planning enriching and educational experiences for his offspring.

Ed's favorite trip was when the six Kruses, both of Evelyn's parents, and her aunt Alvina drove from Brenham to California in the Kruses' green station wagon. It occurred in 1966 when Karen was 15; Ken, 13; Paul, 11, and Neil, 8. One conjures up a vision of the Griswolds heading off to Walley World in *National Lampoon's Vacation*, but Ed remembered it as a fabulous bonding experience that expanded each person's horizons.

One unique feature was that the family cooked a lot of their meals on the road. Because the station wagon had a carry-all on top, they could store their two-burner Coleman stove, the necessary pots and pans, and all the food up there. When they got hungry, they pulled over into a roadside park, got out the cooking gear, prepared the food, and ate. The kids could run around and stretch their legs, and everyone had a break before driving to the next meal, overnight stop, or destination.

The family enjoyed many famous sites along the way, including the Grand Canyon, Marineland of the Pacific, the San Diego Zoo, Disneyland, Death Valley, Las Vegas, the Petrified Forest, Tioga Pass, and Yosemite National Park. Each location they visited could have been a vacation in itself. Ed relished the fact that the family experienced such a variety of venues in one trip.

Of course preparing meals as they traveled from spot to spot meant frequent stops at grocery stores throughout the western part of the United States. While Evelyn went off to purchase milk, cereal, bread, peanut butter, sandwich meat, and other necessities, Ed always headed to the freezer cases with the kids.

He noticed what flavors of ice cream and frozen treats were available. He judged the amount of freezer space allotted to various brands. Attractive displays of product and advertising caught his eye. He surveyed the different types of containers used. Then he bought several small cartons of ice cream and a variety of novelties for the family to share.

Next Ed asked the children their honest opinions of the samples. The replies often indicated that the new products didn't measure up to Blue Bell: "The texture is gummy." "It has a strong artificial taste." "It doesn't melt in my mouth." "It's too icy." "It leaves a strange aftertaste." "It doesn't feel right on my tongue." Sometimes Ed heard favorable comments that he followed up on. He wanted to make sure that Blue Bell made the best products anywhere, even if they were not competing directly with the brands in question.

This adventure out West was educational in even more ways, one of which was unintended. The children were too young to go into the casinos while in Las Vegas, but Ed had a point to prove. He left them with Evelyn, Ewald, and Hildegard, took $20—a lot of money for the family back then—and said he'd return in 30 minutes. Ed expected to lose the $20 and come back with empty pockets and a cautionary tale about the evils of gambling. To his amazement, he tripled his investment. He reappeared on time and honestly reported to the family what had happened. His daughter Karen always respected him for that admission. He could have lied and discussed the futility of gambling. No one would have known the difference. But Ed had the integrity to confess to his good luck and how rare it was. Naturally, the children received the planned lecture anyway.

Another very special vacation took place in Washington, DC. The highlight of that adventure was a visit to the Capitol. Congressman Olin (Tiger) Teague arranged a tour for his fellow Aggie and family. Teague had graduated from Texas A&M in 1932. Serving his country during World War II, Teague participated in the Allied landing at Normandy on D-Day. During the next six months, he achieved such success as a combat soldier that he won more medals than anyone except Audie Murphy, the most decorated soldier in World War II. Teague was severely wounded during the battles, and his injuries caused him to lose part of his left leg. He represented the 6th Congressional District in Texas from 1946 to 1978 and championed veteran's affairs, the space program, and nuclear power.

Congressman Olin Teague's assistant actually conducted the Kruses' personal tour. Ed vividly remembered the enthusiasm of their guide. After each feature he pointed out, the young man would exclaim, "You ain't seen nothin' yet!" The family agreed that they received VIP treatment and an in-depth look at how the US government worked. In the Capitol cafeteria, they ate navy bean soup, which Ed thought most befitting of the occasion.

Other sites visited on the DC excursion included the White House; Williamsburg; Thomas Jefferson's home, Monticello; the Lincoln Memorial; the Smithsonian Institution; and many other famous spots. This trip was necessarily more educational in nature than some of the other Kruse excursions, but Ed and Evelyn wanted the children to visit the seat of the federal government. Evidently, they were not the only parents who thought that way: the capital of the United States was packed with like-thinking families that summer.

The Kruses also took several camping trips while all the children were still at home. Once, they drove to Colorado and stayed in some of the national forests there, as well as at Rocky Mountain National Park. On

Ed and Evelyn Kruse surrounded by their children: clockwise from the left are Paul, Ken, Neil, and Karen. Courtesy of Ed. F. and Evelyn Kruse

this occasion, they traveled in a caravan with a few other families, including Ed's sister Mildred, her husband Dr. Charles Bridges, and their three children. Organized in just a few days, the vacation focused on America's natural beauty and, surprisingly, resulted in their bringing home two chipmunks that the kids caught in a cigar-box trap. The two newcomers joined the Kruse menagerie: the squirrel monkey "Chico," a domesticated crow, about fifty white mice, Ken's boa constrictor, several ducks, a 70-gallon aquarium full of tropical fish, assorted parakeets, guinea pigs, chickens, white rabbits, a gopher, and the boxer "King."

The Kruses headed east another time to camp in the Smoky Mountains. A trip to the northwest found them pitching tents in Yellowstone National Park. While they were in the area, they also camped in Idaho and visited Salt Lake City, Utah. The smell of bacon sizzling over a campfire punctuated these fond memories for Ed.

The vacations were not limited to the United States. Once, the family drove down to Mexico City and then northwest to Guadalajara. They visited many sites between the two cities. This trip may have had an ulterior motive for Ed. A distributor had approached Blue Bell about selling the company's products in Mexico. While they were vacationing, Ed took the opportunity to look at how the wholesaler stocked its stores, the locations of the grocers, the clientele, the competing products, and the condition of the freezer cases. It was a preliminary excursion. Years would pass before Blue Bell sold ice cream south of the border.

Meanwhile the entire family enjoyed the ancient ruins, various historical churches, Mexican markets, museums, delicious food, and the opportunity to be together. The fun ended at the border, however, when the Mexican officials found a trumped-up fault with Ken Kruse's papers. They were obviously expecting Ed to bribe them. Ed was patient as he demonstrated how Ken's papers mirrored those of everyone else, how he resembled the rest of the family, how Ken had been allowed to come into Mexico with them in the first place, and so on. The officials refused to budge. At that point, Ed said, "Okay, keep him!" He turned on his heels and began walking to the car. The stunned agents realized they had lost their own Mexican standoff and sent Ken trotting after his father.

On another excursion, the Kruses flew to St. Croix in the US Virgin Islands and stayed at the Gentle Winds Motel. Since the children had received SCUBA diving lessons and certification at a program at Texas A&M, the Kruses enjoyed SCUBA diving and snorkeling around Buck Island National Park.

Like E. F., Ed took his children fishing on the Gulf coast. They too learned to enjoy the pastime and became proficient anglers. As they were leaving Matagorda after one such excursion, Karen found a kitten and wanted to bring it home. Ed said, "Absolutely not." They had enough animals at home. Karen, knowing the kitten would die unless rescued, sneaked it into the car anyway. She managed to keep it still and quiet—until she fell asleep. At that point, the kitten crawled down from the backseat, clawed its way up the back of the front seat, and nestled on Ed's shoulder as he drove home. "Mattie" found her way into his heart and became another four-legged member of the family.

Even with all this travel, the Ed Kruse children worked at Blue Bell during the summertime. Like their father, their uncle, and their aunts, Karen, Ken, Paul, and Neil grew up in the creamery.

Paul recalls that, when they were barely more than toddlers, they would accompany Ed on "plant checks" at the little creamery on Sunday

Blue Bell Creameries is named after the Texas blue bell. Courtesy of Blue Bell Creameries and Tracey Bryan

afternoons. Their greatest desire was to enter the cold storage room. Ed wouldn't let them—warning that their feet would stick to the floor.

Another job the youngsters performed was collecting used newspapers from neighbors. The entire family would go to the plant, wrap dry ice in the newspapers, and pack large insulated Army bags full of ice cream slices to be served to Fort Hood troops out on maneuvers.

Of course the difficulty of their responsibilities and chores at Blue Bell increased with age—processing ingredients, working in the metal welding shop, answering letters from consumers, helping on the production floor, driving trucks, filing, and much more. Ed Kruse's children became well versed in the family business.

In 1967 Ed and Evelyn bought two acres of land and proceeded to build a new home at 2512 Gun and Rod Road. About four months into the project, they received an excellent offer on their current house on Germania Street. They sold it and moved in with Ed's mother, Bertha Kruse, until the construction was complete. It was an interesting period of time, with Evelyn cooking and cleaning for everyone—and trying to keep the children contained. Fortunately, the original Kruse apartment house was next door, so Evelyn was able to store her furniture there. She even managed to refinish several of the pieces while the children were at school during the day.

The family moved into the brand-new two-story pinkish-tan brick house with white trim as soon as it was completed. There were two bedrooms upstairs—one for Karen and a large "barracks" for the three boys. Ed and Evelyn's bedroom was on the first floor. The home had plenty of room both inside and out. Ed particularly liked the location. It was convenient to Blue Bell, close to both Bertha Kruse and the Tiadens, and not too far from St. Paul's Church, and yet it was outside the city limits and still had a country feel to it.

Ed also enjoyed the fact that the new house was near the Gun and Rod Club where he and Howard had spent countless happy hours swimming, fishing, hunting, and exploring as boys. Now it was convenient for his children to take advantage of those amenities. He coached his kids a bit on their swimming skills at the club's pool, fished with them in the ponds, shot targets with them, and took long walks on the grounds.

The Ed Kruse family was thrilled with their new home and resided there for 35 years. The location proved favorable to Howard Kruse and his family too. They soon built a home next door.

Chapter Thirteen

Don't assume.

(It makes an "ass" out of "u" and "me.")

• EDISM #16 •

ALTHOUGH THE ED KRUSE FAMILY was contently settled in their new spacious home on Gun and Rod Road, the little creamery in Brenham was bursting at the seams. Howard could not discover any additional space on the property on Creamery Street to increase operations to meet the needs of the Houston and Austin markets.

Ed's prediction of the urbanization of Texas had come true. In a speech presented to dairy science students at Texas Tech University on November 10, 1969, Ed, as president of the Dairy Products Institute of Texas, reported that the 1960s began with 9 million Texans, of whom 69 percent lived in cities. The decade was ending with 12 million Texans, with 82 percent urbanized.

Those statistics confirmed that Blue Bell's Houston and Austin markets would continue to grow. Therefore the company developed a plan to build a state-of-the-art plant on 18 acres of land adjoining Loop 577, less than two miles from Ed's and Howard's homes. The property had once been part of the old Brenham airport. Even so, it had no concrete and few improvements. The Brenham Industrial Board had bought it in 1967, hoping to attract industry there. Since then, it had not sold. Ed and Howard thought it might be the ideal location for the new plant, especially considering its proximity to Highway 290, which connects Brenham to both Houston and Austin.

Although 18 acres is a large plot of land for an ice cream plant, Ed and Howard envisioned the additional acreage coming in handy if they ever decided to enter the milk business. In any case, the board of directors

Blue Bell employees in the process of producing "the best ice cream in the country." Courtesy of Blue Bell Creameries

approved the purchase of the land, as well as the construction of a new plant, in January 1970.

Howard worked very closely with the architect Travis Broesche on the design—making sure that each operation would function efficiently. Howard had been in the ice cream manufacturing business long enough to know exactly what he needed and desired. The complex plans further assured the ease of future expansion in three directions—just in case.

In the meantime, Ed arranged the financing. The projected cost was $2 million—a huge amount for the folks at Blue Bell. They would borrow $1.1 million dollars from the Bank of the Southwest in Houston. Ed got a verbal commitment from that lending institution. The rest of the money would come from the $300,000 the company had in cash reserves, $300,000 from the sale of stock, and $300,000 from the sale of debentures, which would later convert to stock.

Current stockholders were offered a certain allotment of shares and debentures. If they decided not to increase their investment in the company, other stockholders took up the slack. Ed invested as much as he could muster in the company at that time and at any other opportunity. Evelyn laughs that people thought they were wealthy because Ed ran Blue Bell. They were actually cash poor, because so much of their income was going back into the company.

Sometimes Ed asked Evelyn not to cash a check until the end of the month. Like many moms, she bought the children's clothes two sizes too big to get more wear out of them. She sewed her own clothes—even the special dresses she wore to conventions. One time, she purchased a dress but hid it under the bed for many weeks. When she finally wore it, Ed complimented her and asked if it were new. She replied, "Oh, no! I've had it a long time!" And so she had!

When the opportunity to buy the debentures to help build the new plant came about, Ed even talked his daughter Karen into using her savings to buy some for herself and her three brothers. He never would have risked her money. It was a wise investment for her. All the stockholders who pitched in to build Blue Bell's new plant reaped the benefits of their sacrifices.

Ed actually started the construction project with the cash Blue Bell already had in reserve in the bank. He did not want to pay any more interest on a loan than was absolutely necessary. The ground had been broken and construction begun when Ed called up the president of the Bank of the Southwest in Houston to set up an appointment to formalize the $1.1 million loan.

The banker replied, "Ed, we've been thinking. We don't know how to run an ice cream plant." Ed asked what he meant. The response was, "Well, we know how to run a motel, a restaurant, or something, but we don't know how to run an ice cream plant." It finally dawned on Ed that Bank of the Southwest was not going to loan Blue Bell the money it needed to complete the new facility. The banker did say that the loan committee would reconsider if Blue Bell built the plant in Houston.

Changing locations was not an option: construction was ongoing. Besides, Brenham folks had been completely responsible for the success of the company so far. Ed was going to stick to the plan. Nevertheless, the bank's reneging on the understood agreement was, according to Ed, "the biggest challenge and headache I ever had." Ed spent almost three days virtually without sleep. He was constantly on the phone talking to local banks, savings and loans, and insurance companies—determined to line up the credit he needed.

Whereas the Bank of the Southwest could have supplied the entire loan, the smaller entities had tighter limits, so a joint effort was required.

Because the First National Bank of Brenham needed to be kept out of the picture since it provided short-term operative loans to Blue Bell, Washington County State Bank took the lead and handled the paperwork. Also included in the agreement were Farmers National Bank, Bank of Somerville, Bank of Bellville, Bank of Sealy, and Brenham Savings and Loan. Once he secured the necessary credit, Ed had a great sense of pride and satisfaction in doing business with local banking institutions that knew and trusted him and vice versa.

In July 1972 one of the largest and most modern ice cream plants in the world opened in the small community of Brenham, Texas. It featured a 45,000-square-foot production area, a mixing room, a cold-storage warehouse, and a 5,000-square-foot masonry business office. The new plant had the ability to manufacture 8 million gallons of ice cream annually. E. F. Kruse would have been absolutely overwhelmed—and delighted—by its efficiency and capacity.

On the other hand, the new facility did not completely replace the "little creamery in Brenham." Located on Creamery Street, the original plant continued to produce frozen snacks. In addition, those trusting banking entities in Central Texas quickly had their loans repaid from the income generated from increased production and sales.

To assist Howard in running the new plant, Blue Bell hired Eugene Supak, a graduate in dairy science from Texas A&M. Ed and Howard recruited Gene immediately upon graduation, but the young man decided he could make more money with Carnation. The brothers countered that Blue Bell would be happy to hire him if he ever changed his mind. After an out-of-state stint with Carnation and service in Vietnam, Gene called Ed and asked if he still had a position open for him. Ed assured him he did, and Gene began working at Blue Bell on February 1, 1971. He proved to be an outstanding asset to the company.

An engineer at heart, Gene could alter existing machines to perform new functions. He also had a knack for buying machinery at auction for cents on the dollar and integrating it into the Blue Bell system. Some of Blue Bell's most advanced and innovative frozen snacks were the result of Gene's vivid imagination. Gene came to the company in the formative stages of the new plant; he oversaw expansions, renovations, new construction, and eventually operations for the next 40 years.

Gene must have wondered what he had gotten himself into when there was an ammonia leak in the brand new plant on July 12, 1973. As one of the employees prepared to go home that Thursday afternoon, he heard a pop and smelled the distinctive odor of anhydrous ammonia, the common coolant used at ice cream plants. The facilities were immediately evacuated, and the ammonia valve switched off. Fortunately, there were no injuries and the ammonia did not explode, which is possible under certain circumstances. Wearing protective masks, employees worked all weekend to move contaminated ice cream to the landfill.

In the meantime, Howard searched for the cause of the leak. He feared that the entire plant might have similar defects. Finally, he discovered that one of the line caps had not been properly welded and annealed. It had blown off under pressure. Fixing that problem and checking the rest of the system, the plant was declared safe—and totally sound. Thanks to the dedication and hard work of many Blue Bell employees, production was back on line the following Monday morning.

If the call to the Bank of the Southwest brought about the greatest crisis Ed had to deal with at Blue Bell, the ammonia leak was Howard's equivalent. The two very capable brothers, by this time in their 40s, proved they were up to the challenges, and the excellent Blue Bell team rose to the occasion as well.

Ed's exceptional hires also stood out in other areas. Ed brought John Barnhill back to Brenham from Houston to run the entire departments of sales and advertising. Larry Ainsworth succeeded John as Houston's very capable branch manager. Other young men in the Houston sales force were readying themselves for advancement.

One prime example was Melvin Ziegenbein, who had served in various positions in Houston, Austin, and Brenham. When Carnation came to Ed in 1973 and offered Blue Bell an entry into the Beaumont area, Ed jumped at the chance. Blue Bell would take over Carnation's two and a half ice cream delivery routes, its branch office, and its cold storage facility for a year, the only costs being the electricity and the purchase of some ice cream cases. This proposal would give Blue Bell a chance to try the new market before totally committing to it. After all, Beaumont was 156 miles east of Brenham, and the company needed to see how operations would function at that distance. Melvin Ziegenbein was Ed's choice to run the experiment.

Melvin proved himself up to the task, even under very difficult circumstances, including a roof that leaked "like a sieve" into part of the cold storage area. After each rain, Melvin would arrive to find 3 to 4 inches of ice on the floor and have to chop it with a pickax. He managed that situation and the entire regional office very well. Under Melvin's leadership, Blue Bell established its third branch in Beaumont. Because the location was close to Louisiana, some of the Blue Bell products even inched out of the state of Texas—maybe a sign of things to come.

Ed Kruse meanwhile faced another frustrating challenge. He had been accustomed to the price of sugar averaging about 18 cents per pound, and Blue Bell bought a lot of sugar. In 1974 pressures on the world market caused the wholesale price to rise precipitously. One week the price grew to 30 cents per pound; the next, 40 cents per pound. The price finally reached 72 cents per pound. At each increase, Ed raised the retail prices of the Blue Bell products. At times, the company's items were increasing every two weeks. He faced sharp criticism inside the company and out, but he was determined that Blue Bell was not going to go broke. He knew that once the market madness settled, he could bring the prices back down. He had to trust that consumers would continue to buy Blue Bell Ice Cream and realize that, at Blue Bell, "We want to give value. We're not going to overprice, and we're not going to underprice. *Period.*"

As it turned out, Ed's response to the crisis worked. The consumers saw other items containing sugar increasing in price and read in the newspapers about the historically high costs. True, some ice cream fans had to cut back their purchases, but Blue Bell didn't receive any ill will from Ed's approach to the temporary conditions.

Although the price of sugar was an exceptional condition, double-digit inflation and unemployment plagued the national economy in the 1970s. Blue Bell, of course, suffered along with everyone else. The company did not resort to layoffs, but expenditures were monitored ever more carefully.

To make matters worse, governmental regulation on all levels was "wasteful, duplicative and costly." As president of the Dairy Products Institute of Texas, Ed urged attendees at a Southwestern Dairy Industry Conference in 1970 to get involved in the political arena and let candidates know the hardships plaguing the food sector of the economy. Measures of uniformity and communication between the various governmental powers would alleviate the pressure on the dairy companies.

The dairy industry also faced stiff competition from imitations and substitute products. Oleomargarine and mellorine featured vegetable oils instead of milk products. In a similar vein, artificial sweeteners began to replace sugar in several products. Here, Ed resisted legislative solutions in favor of allowing the consumer to make the choice.

Ed also encouraged the dairy industry to seek innovative products. He gave the example of yogurt, which was practically unheard of in the mid-1960s but had an ever-increasing following. To quote Ed, "Low fat milk, diet frozen desserts and milk-based instant breakfasts are examples of imaginative thinking in product development."

Ed Kruse prepares to speak to a gathering of the Texas Dairy Institute when he was president of that organization. Courtesy of Ed. F. and Evelyn Kruse

Furthermore, Ed reminded several audiences during the 1970s of the importance of milk products to human nutrition. Because of their high essential protein, "milk, ice cream and other dairy products are nature's most nearly perfect food." And, considering cost, "Pound for pound, dairy products are the housewife's best food buy."

One other concern emerged in Ed's talks before various dairy groups he headed in the 1970s: the poor image of private business and free enterprise. He referred to a survey of US college students. It reported that 90 percent of the respondents thought that business was too profit minded, that it stifled initiative, that it was too conforming, and that it was conducted without principle. In that same poll, only 12 percent of college graduates said they would consider a job in the business sector. Ed personally considered the results of the survey skewed. Nevertheless, it seemed ironic to him that US students felt dispirited about American innovation and small business, while the USSR was beginning to understand the value of incentives and bonuses for its factory workers who excelled at their jobs.

Communication held the key. Ed urged, "We, in business, must take to the people a strong, clear case that the privately owned business is an invention vital to their welfare and that our economic system is the best way for a free people to bring about their own economic well-being, to support their intellectual, spiritual and cultural aspirations, and to guarantee their basic individual freedoms."

Ed must have felt like he was constantly putting out fires in the first seven or eight years of the 1970s. Yet as difficult as those times were, he succeeded again and again. He began to think that maybe he did know a little bit about running an ice cream company, and he developed, or co-opted, a few bits of wisdom to explain his approach to others.

For example, his dealings with the Bank of the Southwest were telling. Even though a handshake in Texas had always indicated a firm word, Ed realized that he had been naïve. One should never assume; as he said, it makes an "ass" out of "u" and "me." From 1970 on, he signed all his agreements in writing.

An Edism corollary to the loan experience would be "You can whip almost any problem if you work hard enough and long enough." As traumatized as Ed was when the Bank of the Southwest loan fell through, he jumped into action to solve the problem. It took 72 hours to line up the alternative financing, but he succeeded.

In another instance, despite the criticisms Ed experienced when he continued to raise ice cream prices in line with increased sugar costs, he maintained his practice of giving consumers an excellent product at a good value. He had always believed that one should "be honest in your dealings." He remained true to his beliefs and weathered the storm.

Ed's pleasure at the new team members he had hired at Blue Bell could be summed up in his saying, "Aptitude is important, but so is attitude." He recognized enthusiasm, work ethic, eagerness to learn and grow, and excellent character in many of the people who applied for jobs. Those qualities often took precedence over the skills they brought to the table. Job requirements could be taught to avid learners. Moreover, these willing participants would be much more likely to bring innovation to the workplace.

At that point, Ed possibly became a little *too* confident in his ability to manage the company. In 1976 he designed a frozen snack on a stick that he just knew would spur sales tremendously. He called it the Jelly Terror, and it consisted of "a tart strawberry jelly center encased in rich vanilla ice milk with a chocolate covering." Ed had a batch made up and loved it. He went through the formalities of presenting it to the sales team and having them vote on it. To a man, the product was voted down. Ed refused to believe their opinions, figuring they just didn't have a pulse on the market for such an innovative product. Therefore he made an executive decision and had the Jelly Terror made and distributed. It turned out that Ed was the one out of touch. He joked that he ate practically every last one of the "jelly terrible" treats.

Ed insisted that he was just ahead of a trend—one which still hasn't materialized. Fortunately for the consumers of Blue Bell Ice Cream, Ed decided to leave product development to Howard and his team. That decision was a good thing: a great new flavor was in the works.

Chapter Fourteen

Do what you say you're going to do.

• EDISM #26 •

THE STORY GOES that one of the Blue Bell sales team was in Florida on vacation. He had extra time at the airport so he wandered into an ice cream shop, where one of the combinations available was crushed bits of Oreo cookies mixed in with vanilla ice cream. Choosing that option, he found the flavor absolutely delicious and wondered if Howard could produce something similar in cartons, rather than one cone at a time.

Howard accepted the challenge, and after months of experimenting, he developed Blue Bell Cookies 'n Cream. In 1978 the company introduced the new flavor in 3-gallon containers for use in ice cream parlors. Howard didn't initially sell Cookies 'n Cream in half-gallons, because producing the flavor was very labor-intensive. Nabisco, the company that made Oreos, refused to sell them in bulk or in large packages to Blue Bell. Therefore plant employees had to open consumer-sized packages one by one and place the cookies into a grinding machine to be crushed before being mixed with the vanilla ice cream. However, the new flavor was so popular that in 1980 Howard relented, and the half-gallon cartons flew out of the grocers' freezer cases.

Howard had another hit: whereas his Homemade Vanilla stands at the top of Blue Bell's sales, Cookies 'n Cream is the second biggest bestseller. In both cases, Blue Bell was the first ice cream company in the United States to produce cartons of the remarkable flavors. Many others plants followed Blue Bell's lead.

Cookies 'n Cream proved to be only one of the successes at the end of the 1970s. Howard Kruse and Gene Supak also began making the first three-dimensional frozen snacks in the country. Plump little lions, rabbits, monkeys, and bears in fudge ice cream or chocolate-covered vanilla ice cream appeared on the scene. The animal shapes also came in cherry, orange, or lemon-flavored ices. New equipment from the DCA Food Industries in New York made these Animal Fun Shapes possible. Many companies had produced flat cut-out figures: Blue Bell itself had been the first in Texas to make such novelties as the Big Brown Clown and the Mouseketeer Bar. However, the three-dimensionality of the Animal Fun Shapes made them unique.

Howard Kruse produced another hit when he developed Blue Bell Cookies 'n Cream Ice Cream in 1978. Courtesy of Blue Bell Creameries

Blue Bell's list of "firsts" in the late 1970s/early 1980s also included being the first plant in Texas to manufacture frozen yogurt and the first to offer take-home packages of six or twelve frozen snacks. The creative minds in Blue Bell's plant operations achieved many innovations.

Because of Blue Bell's successful sales, grocery store chains in the Houston and Austin markets encouraged Ed to offer the company's products in their stores in the Dallas area. Much to Waco's disappointment at being skipped over, Ed opted to take the plunge.

John Barnhill and Lyle Metzdorf agreed with Ed's decision, but they felt that Blue Bell needed a little more sophistication in its country image before entering the Dallas market. Lyle began working on a fresh logo to replace the bell that adorned Blue Bell's packaging and advertising. He finally recommended the image of a little girl leading her Jersey cow.

Ed admitted that it took him about a year to agree to the new logo. He considered the change a huge decision. The bell had symbolized the company for many years and had brought brand identification. Then there was the fact that cows have four teats. Every drawing Lyle showed him displayed only three, one being assumed to be behind the others. Finally in 1977, Lyle came up with an image that showed all four teats and satisfied both him and Ed. The cow and girl logo maintained the country-based image that had been so successful for Blue Bell. It ushered Blue Bell into the Dallas market and remains the very recognizable symbol of the company today.

At about the same time, Blue Bell came up with the idea of having different colored rims—white, gold, and silver. Of Blue Bell's ice cream, some of the flavors had ingredients that cost more than others. The flavors with the gold rim tops contained the most expensive ingredients, so the

Lyle Metzdorf created Blue Bell's cow and girl logo as the company prepared to enter the Dallas market. Courtesy of Blue Bell Creameries

consumer was charged a little more, maybe 10 cents per carton over the silver rim, which was about 10 cents per carton more than the white rim. The company instituted this practice before going into Dallas.

To lead Blue Bell's entry into the new market, Ed turned to Melvin Ziegenbein once again. Melvin had performed exceedingly well in Beaumont and in every other position he had held at Blue Bell. Ed felt confident about his abilities to introduce Blue Bell Ice Cream to the Dallas area.

Ziegenbein had a long history with Blue Bell. Melvin had worked part-time for the company in Houston while he was studying for his degree in mathematics at Texas A&M. After he graduated in 1966, he interviewed with Ed Kruse for a full-time job. Ed definitely wanted to hire him as a territory manager in Austin, but Blue Bell could not match the offer Melvin was receiving from IBM in Huntsville, Alabama. Melvin displayed much loyalty to Blue Bell when he accepted the position in Austin, rather than the higher-paying IBM proposal.

Ed reciprocated the loyalty when Melvin was called up to serve his country in Vietnam only three months later. Upon Melvin's return in 1968, Ed had a position waiting for him in Houston. In 1971 Ed made him sales manager in Brenham. In that job, Melvin supervised two veteran salespeople—Andy Anderson and Vastine Pietsch. Melvin handled the temporarily disgruntled old-timers with grace and aplomb. Subsequently, he endured the frozen floors in Beaumont when he became branch manager there beginning in 1973. After his superb performance as operations manager in Houston beginning in 1975, Ed knew Melvin could manage just about any situation.

Meanwhile, Houston—Branch #1—remained under the excellent management of Larry Ainsworth. Clarence Jaster thrived in his position over Branch #2 in Austin. And Branch #3—Beaumont—was now run by Travis Brewer, a Brenham "boy," who had once been in Ed Kruse's Boy Scout troop. Travis had joined Blue Bell in 1972 and had achieved a meteoric rise to become branch manager. Even though he had a college education, Travis's achievements were primarily the result of an upbeat attitude and just plain hard work, attributes Ed Kruse always admired.

In 1978 Melvin eagerly accepted the position as manager of Blue Bell's Branch #4 in Dallas. For budget purposes, Ed asked the talented mathematician to establish a monthly forecast of sales for the first year in Dallas. Melvin went a step further and came up with a 52-week projection of $2.7 million in sales. Ed felt that Melvin had overestimated the market and was placing too much pressure on himself. Ed reduced the expected amount to $2.5 million. When the end of the year arrived, Melvin had been right on target: Blue Bell garnered $2.7 million in sales that first year in Dallas.

Moreover, with Dallas added to the mix, Blue Bell's increase in sales in the year 1979 was a whopping 31 percent over sales in 1978. For 1980 the company projected sales of $41 million. A mere 10 years before, $5 million in sales had been the goal.

When Ed Kruse sat down with Floyd Jenkins of North Texas State University (now the University of North Texas) to do a thorough oral history for the school's Business Archives Project on August 18, 1981, Ed had additional good news to report. Blue Bell's dollar sales had increased 36 percent in 1980 over 1979, and 1981 sales were already 35 percent ahead of those in 1980. Besides that, Blue Bell had 54.8 percent of the ice cream market share in Houston, 46 percent in Beaumont and Austin, and 14 percent in Dallas/Fort Worth after selling product there for only two and a half years. That 14 percent was the largest share of any ice cream brand in the Dallas/Fort Worth territory.

With all this activity, Blue Bell increasingly received attention in the press. One of the many examples was an article in the *Texas Department of Agriculture Quarterly* in 1981. It gave a brief history of the company and focused on the innovative machinery Howard had added to the production line. The author quoted Ed's formula for success: "A quality product with the best ingredients and great people." Further noted was the fact that 58 percent of the company's employees who worked for Blue Bell in 1951, when Ed became manager, remained on the job 30 years later.

In 1983 the *Dallas Morning News* published a feature article describing an informative and mouth-watering tour of the creamery. It further discussed how Lyle Metzdorf had based some of the company's ads on comments Blue Bell received in correspondence from its consumers. The letter the article cited said, "Dear Blue Bell: Guess your ice cream is good 'cause the cows think Brenham is Heaven."

Hitting the national scene, Blue Bell earned mention in a lengthy article on ice cream in *Time* magazine on August 10, 1981. Writer John Skow gave only a brief reference to the little creamery in Brenham, but it was high praise: "Forget all this and resolve the next time you are in Texas to obtain the best ice cream in the world, which is made by Blue Bell Creameries of Washington County, between Austin and Houston."

Appreciating the recognition, Ed Kruse kept his nose to the grindstone. He brought two more essential members to the Blue Bell team in the early 1980s. Bill Rankin became Ed's financial administrative assistant and eventual chief financial officer. Bill grew up in Brenham and excelled in high school. Accepted into the Air Force Academy, he returned to Texas A&M after a year because he wanted to marry his longtime girlfriend Lois Langehennig. Bill was chosen as outstanding sophomore in the Corps of Cadets, graduated magna cum laude with a degree in accounting, and earned his CPA. Still owing the Air Force years of service, Bill became a pilot and flight instructor. Ed laughs at the simple lesson Bill reportedly taught his students: "You go into an airplane and you pull the stick back and things get smaller. You push the stick forward and things on the ground get bigger. You're either going up or you're going down."

Ed had been observing Bill's progress since high school. At one point, Bill was stationed in Del Rio. Later he transferred to Keflavik, Iceland. After six months, the Air Force offered him his choice of any base in the world if he would re-enlist for three years. Bill chose to finish his current commitment of six more months and was promptly sent back to Iceland.

On a furlough in Brenham, Bill and Ed ran into each other at the golf club. Bill really impressed Ed—not just because of his inspiring 8 handicap, but because he took the time to talk to Ed for about 10 minutes—Ed himself was usually too focused on his game to stop for a visit. Ed knew that Bill would make an amazing Blue Bell employee.

As closely as Ed had followed Bill, the young man slipped through his fingers when he finished his Air Force duty and accepted a job with a CPA firm in Brenham. The accountant Ed had hired from Houston had recently returned to the larger city, and Ed really wanted Bill for that job. Ed ran into Bill's brother Bob Rankin and mentioned that he was looking for an accountant if he happened to know one. Bob, one of Brenham's leading insurance men, didn't really respond to the comment. A few weeks later, Ed saw Bob again and stated, "Bob, I'm still looking for a good CPA." Bob replied, "My brother's a CPA." Ed responded with a surprised lilt in his voice, "He *is*? *Really*? Please tell him I've got an opening up here that he might be interested in. It won't cost him anything to come up and just interview with me."

When Bill came to talk to Ed, Ed told him all about the job, its perks, and even the salary. He ended the interview with a job offer. Bill must have wondered how Ed could have come to such a quick conclusion about him. He didn't realize that Ed had been following his career for years. Bill asked for a few days to think about the position and to discuss it with Lois. The first thing the next morning, Bill called Ed and accepted the job. He said, "Mr. Kruse, I don't know what I was thinking about. I feel like I've been drafted by the Dallas Cowboys!" Bill gave proper notice to the CPA firm and has been an essential contributing member of the Blue Bell team ever since.

Another excellent hire made in the 1980s also took some watching and waiting on Ed's part. This young man achieved status as salutatorian of his Brenham High School class. He majored in accounting at Texas A&M and graduated in 1977 as a distinguished student. Afterward, he attended Baylor University School of Law, where he served on the staff of the *Baylor Law Review* and was president of the law students' association. Ed needed legal counsel at Blue Bell, so he offered the young man—his son Paul Kruse—an opportunity to join the team.

Having always been encouraged to follow his own passion and his own line of work by his dad, Paul had already accepted a year's clerkship with Judge Austin O. McCloud, Chief Justice of the Eleventh Court of Civil Appeals in Eastland, Texas. Judge McCloud, knowing Paul's connection to a family business, had asked Paul in the interview if he really planned on following through on a clerkship. Paul assured him of his commitment to the job, received the judge's offer, and served with such distinction that Judge McCloud asked him to stay for another year.

By that time, Paul had made plans to go into practice in Brenham with his friend, Bill Betts. Bill had followed in his father's footsteps, so he already had an office and a law library. All Paul would need to purchase was a desk. He would also pay half of the secretary's salary.

Ed said to his son, "You know I'd like to have you at Blue Bell. I've got to have a lawyer."

Paul replied, "No I can't do it. I've already told Bill I'd work with him. I went to school to practice law, and that's what I'm going to do." Ed acquiesced.

In 1983 the board of directors at Blue Bell elected Paul Kruse to become a member of the board. Two years later, Ed Kruse felt that he desperately needed legal counsel at Blue Bell. He approached Paul again, told him the situation, and admitted that Paul was his first choice. He further stated, "I don't want to put any pressure on you—one way or another. I'd like to have you, but at the same token, if you're happy in your law practice, I want you to be where you're happy. *Period.* You've got to pursue your passion, and that's it." Paul said that he would think about his father's proposition.

Six weeks went by, and Paul said nothing. Finally, Ed asked Paul if he had made a decision. Paul said that he had thought about his dad's offer and would join Blue Bell under two conditions: The first was that no one would be told yet that he was going to quit his law practice to work for Blue Bell. Paul felt obligated to finish the commitment to his current clients, but he would not take on any new cases. The second requirement was that he be given an entire year to wind up his law practice. Ed agreed to hold the position open for Paul. In 1986, Paul Kruse joined Blue Bell as its legal counsel and also became corporate secretary. Ed remarked that Paul was his toughest hire ever.

By 1986 it seemed fairly clear that Ed's other three children would not be making their careers with Blue Bell Creameries. First-born Karen had graduated from Brenham High School in 1969, from Blinn College in 1971, and from Texas A&M in 1973. She was the first student to receive a degree in medical technology from Texas A&M. Karen continued her education at Baylor University Medical Center at Dallas and the University of Texas at Dallas in the late 1970s. She also studied for her real estate broker's license and received it in 1983. In the meantime, she had married David A. Bosse, MD, in 1974, and they were busy rearing a family: Michael was born in 1977; Melissa came along in 1979; Stephen arrived in 1982; and Sarah was born in 1987.

Ken Kruse, the second of Ed's and Evelyn's children, also attended Brenham schools and Texas A&M. He graduated with a degree in dairy science and worked at Blue Bell for a few years. Eventually realizing that the ice cream business was not his calling, Ken moved to Austin to attend the University of Texas so that he could take courses that would prepare him for either medical school or dental school. Upon finishing the requirements, Ken was accepted at the University of Texas Dental School in Houston. He graduated with his DDS in 1986, at which time he established a practice in general dentistry in Houston.

Paul followed Ken in birth order, and Neil was the baby of the family. Neil, like his siblings, attended the Brenham public schools and Texas A&M University. After he earned his bachelor's degree in 1980, Neil was accepted in the dentistry program at the University of Texas Health Science Center in San Antonio. Upon graduating with his DDS in 1984, Neil returned to Brenham and set up a practice. That same year, he married his longtime sweetheart Janie Koester of Houston. Neil became his father's dentist and developed a large practice in the community. Ed Kruse attributed Neil's popularity to the fact that Neil was very confident, competent, and painless in his approach to dental work.

With all his children set on their own life journeys, Ed decided to shift some titles and responsibilities at Blue Bell in 1986. After E. F. Kruse died in 1951, Ed had become general manager and secretary/treasurer of Blue

Bell Creameries. The president of the company was Herbert C. Hohlt, a Brenham businessman and the son of H. F. Hohlt, one of the founders. Soon after Howard's arrival, Howard became assistant general manager. Herbert Hohlt died in 1968, at which point Ed assumed the additional titles of president and chairman of the board with the approval of the board of directors. At the same time, Howard's title became assistant general manager and secretary. The board of directors added vice president to Howard's title in 1980.

In 1986 Ed decided to cut his days at the office from five to four. Perhaps being in the plane crash in Presidio, Texas, in February 1984 had been a wake-up call for him to slow down a bit. Regardless, he wanted to give Howard more practice in handling the overall day-to-day operations of the company. Ed therefore became chief executive officer and remained chairman of the board. Howard assumed the title of president; Paul became secretary and Bill Rankin treasurer of the company. Ed must have felt very content to have both his own children and his Blue Bell family on firm footing for the future.

Chapter Fifteen

It's a cinch by the inch, hard by the yard.

• EDISM #11 •

IN 1980 BLUE BELL had four branches outside of Brenham. All of them—Houston, Austin, Beaumont, and Dallas—were in Texas. Twenty years later, the little creamery in Brenham featured thirty-four branches in twelve states. The production needed to handle these markets would be helped by two additional plants—one in Broken Arrow, Oklahoma, and the other in Sylacauga, Alabama.

What seems like phenomenal growth was planned very methodically. Ed Kruse called it the "Blue Bell Way." He admitted that the process had evolved over time because he learned from mistakes made in the early markets. For example, the building for the initial branch in Houston turned out to be too small. Blue Bell ended up buying the property next door to the branch and adding on to the building several times. Ed had no idea that the number of routes out of that regional office would quickly increase to twenty.

Some of the new branches came about simply as a way to relieve pressure on already existing distribution centers. Alvin, between Houston and Galveston, became the location of Branch #5. It took some of the routes from the Houston branch and added others on the nearby Texas Gulf Coast. Similarly, Branch #6 in Fort Worth relieved the Dallas branch of some of its routes while it concentrated on new sales in the areas west of Dallas.

Ed gave John Barnhill credit for establishing the structure for a perfect branch. Basically, the branch manager and three territorial managers develop and promote sales. Each territorial manager has six driver-salesmen under him to service customers—grocery stores, convenient stores, schools, hospitals, restaurants, and other entities—on the routes. John felt that the optimum number of routes for a branch was eighteen.

When it came to deciding where Blue Bell would expand, Ed kept two thoughts in mind. He looked for significant centers of population, and he deliberately sought areas contiguous to those Blue Bell was already serving. Usually the decisions were prompted by successful sales in current grocery store chains, that also had locations in nearby areas. The slow creeping into new territories reflected Ed's saying at Blue Bell: "It's a cinch by the inch, hard by the yard."

Additional new branches in the 1980s followed these trends.

Branch #7—North Dallas—1982—relieved pressure on the Dallas branch and expanded routes north of the city

Branch #8—Humble—1982—relieved pressure on the Houston branch and expanded routes north of that city

Branch #9—San Antonio—1984—took good sales in the Austin area and expanded them further south

Branch #10—South Dallas—1985—relieved pressure on the Dallas branch and expanded routes south of the city

Branch #11—East Texas—1986—expanded sales east from Dallas into the Longview/Tyler area

Branch #12—Waco—1986—finally closed the gap between Austin and Dallas. Waco had been waiting for years for Blue Bell to arrive in its community. The bootlegging of Blue Bell Ice Cream from Austin and Dallas—and even Hillsboro and Temple—could halt. It's even been reported that Waco consumers brought spoons with them to the grocery store to eat their Blue Bell Ice Cream while they were standing in the checkout line. They had waited long enough.

Branch #13—Corpus Christi—1988—was near enough to San Antonio to have many of the same grocery stores for Blue Bell sales

Branch #14—Oklahoma City, Oklahoma—1989—was the first out-of-state branch, but it developed out of sales in north Texas

Branch #15—Baton Rouge, Louisiana—1989—followed grocery store chains whose market areas crossed the Sabine River east of Longview

With all this growth, Howard continued expanding the plant in Brenham. That necessitated hiring new personnel and training them properly to ensure the quality of Blue Bell's products. Howard had excellent programs in place to instruct people in the company's manufacturing processes. Whether they were graduates of Texas A&M's dairy science program, had received a degree in mechanical engineering from a university, came with manufacturing experience from other companies, had technical training elsewhere, or had little experience but a great desire to learn and grow—it didn't matter. Everyone in the plant was thoroughly taught the "Blue Bell Way" of doing things.

Gone were the days when employees sometimes had to fly by the seat of their pants. Many of the oldest plant operators had grown up on farms where they were often on their own and had to make do with baling wire, glue, and other improvisations to solve mechanical problems. These skills aided in Blue Bell's success, because the men were accustomed to managing in a crisis. Some of Blue Bell's innovations and unique processes stemmed directly from their input. But the plant was now more sophisticated, and the new employees arrived with different sets of talents to contribute. Howard's training courses took these variances into consideration, and the employees and the company benefited greatly.

Leeroy Kramer could attest to that. He was hired to work in the plant by E. F. Kruse in 1949. He was another smart, diligent worker who moved up through the ranks to become plant manager. As Reinhardt Loesch began to step back, Leeroy and Kervin Finke gradually took over the duties of running the plant. Leeroy ran the new factory after it was completed in 1972 while Kervin stayed in charge of the "little creamery." Despite his obvious success, Leeroy didn't receive nearly the thorough training as those who followed him. He often had to improvise on the job. When Leeroy retired in 1995, after 46 years with Blue Bell, he admitted that Howard's methods of training and precision worked. In Kramer's opinion, the best asset of the company was the quality of the products. He remarked, "We consistently make our product the same way every time. I just don't see how any other company could do that."

The same hiring and training took place in the area of sales. The members of this team often studied a number of different disciplines in college. Ed felt that having a degree was important because it demonstrated the ability to stick to a plan and accomplish a difficult and long-range goal. With these assets, a great attitude, and an eagerness to work hard, Blue Bell could train a new employee for a sales position.

Ed Kruse also admired those with little or no college background who kept rising in the company. A prime example was James Liepke, who started as a route salesman in Houston, moved up to route supervisor, became a territorial manager, progressed to sales manager, and eventually became the branch manager in Humble. Later he volunteered to head the new branch in Baton Rouge and retired as a regional manager over six branches. James didn't have the same formal education that most of the people in his position did. However, he was very outgoing, worked smart and diligently, and had a sense of true joy for his job.

When Ed Kruse asked James Liepke if he would take the sideways move from being branch manager in Humble, where he had established deep roots, to the same position in Baton Rouge, James didn't hesitate to answer, "Yes." He continued, "Mr. Kruse, you've been so good to me. You don't have to ask me to go. You just have to tell me, and I'll do it."
Ed challenged him, "What if I wanted you to go to New York City?"

James replied, "I'd go."

What touched Ed most was when James described Blue Bell as his family. "I had a dad who was crippled, and my mom worked all the time. My two sisters were long gone when I was growing up, so I really didn't have a family-type atmosphere. Now I do."

Ed was pleased that James retired to Dallas, where he enjoyed playing a lot of golf. Ed admitted that James didn't have much opportunity to participate in leisure pastimes when he was working hard for Blue Bell.

The combination of very well qualified candidates, superb training, excellent opportunities to prove oneself, strong and supportive supervisors who kept an eye out for outstanding performance, and a company that was expanding was a fortunate one. Blue Bell had always striven to promote talent from within, and with new branches and plants coming aboard in the 1980s and 1990s, opportunity abounded for the company's employees.

The new branches in the 1990s included Tulsa, Oklahoma; Big Spring in West Texas; New Orleans, Louisiana; Harlingen in the Rio Grande Valley of Texas; Ruston, Louisiana; Kansas City, Kansas; Mobile, Alabama; Jackson, Mississippi; Montgomery, Alabama; Birmingham, Alabama; Little Rock, Arkansas; Huntsville, Alabama; New Braunfels, Texas; Atlanta, Georgia (two branches); Lewisville in North Texas; Memphis, Tennessee; and Lafayette, Louisiana.

It might seem that Blue Bell reached out of contiguous territory in this vast expansion of sales area in the 1990s. However, two additional manufacturing facilities allowed the company to move according to its original plan. Blue Bell built a brand-new plant in Broken Arrow, Oklahoma, to help supply its North Texas and Oklahoma markets and to reach farther into the Midwest. That plant began operations in October 1992.

In this case, Ed and Howard Kruse didn't just wake up one day in 1991 and decide to construct a plant in Oklahoma. Ed recalled, "When we built the new manufacturing plant in Broken Arrow, Oklahoma, we were training people five years ahead of time in order to meet our anticipated need.

Blue Bell first produced ice cream outside the state of Texas when it opened a plant in Broken Arrow, Oklahoma, in 1992. Courtesy of Blue Bell Creameries

They needed to be qualified to carry our operation successfully into a new area. So we have tried to define our growth pattern as far in advance as possible and promote and move people accordingly."

The $10 million dollar Broken Arrow plant opened with 123,000 square feet and about 100 employees; later expansions could provide for as many as 250 employees. Centrally located between St. Louis, Oklahoma City, Kansas City, and Dallas, the new plant would focus on Midwest sales. It allowed the plant in Brenham to concentrate on Texas and the southeastern United States.

The Sylacauga plant was not planned so far in advance—or at all, really. However, circumstances brought it online quickly. In 1996, Land O' Sun Dairy of Johnson, Tennessee, closed its Flav-O-Rich ice cream plant in the small community of Sylacauga, Alabama. One of the 136 employees who were laid off was Pete Moore, the former plant operations manager at the facility. He called Blue Bell to see if the Texas company had any interest in purchasing a manufacturing plant that could help supply its expanding market into the southeastern part of the United States.

Howard Kruse and Gene Supak had never totally renovated a plant, but after careful study and planning, they felt that they could conform the facility to Blue Bell's exacting standards. They hired many of the former employees of Flav-O-Rich to help with the extensive improvements, and a state-of-the-art plant resulted. It began production in May 1997, with a handful of Blue Bell personnel and many of those same Flav-O-Rich employees running the production lines. Howard and Gene made sure the personnel were thoroughly trained in Blue Bell's method of manufacturing and quality control. Having a plant in that part of the country helped Blue Bell expand more efficiently into the Southeast and along the Atlantic coast. It also shortened the distance for many tractor-trailer trips between plants and branches.

One aspect of the "Blue Bell Way" is to control products meticulously from the time the dairy commodities and other ingredients arrive at the company and throughout the entire manufacturing process. Under the company's direct store delivery system (DSD), Blue Bell further ensures optimal temperature of its ice cream and frozen snacks during their transportation to the branches in Blue Bell's tractor-trailer trucks, while in storage at the branches, when being delivered to the stores in Blue Bell's bobtail trucks, and until placed in the grocers' freezer cases.

As Ed remarked to a reporter from *Refrigerated Transport* in 1969, "Ice cream is probably the most sensitive product in the frozen foods field. A case or carton of frozen peas could probably sit on a loading dock for a couple of hours without any apparent change to quality, but ice cream is different. The change of just a few degrees means heat shock." Ed and Howard insisted that Blue Bell's DSD system accompanied the expansion of the sales territories and maintained its products in perfect condition.

In 1998 Ed recounted, "My dad always told me, 'Don't think small.' I don't think even he dreamed we'd be in twelve states today. We moved a lot faster than either he or I thought. On the other hand, we could be larger than we are now if we had chosen to change our distribution methods. But that was a deliberate decision to take a stand for controlling quality and delivering all products with our own personnel and trucks."

When Ed spoke these words near the end of the twentieth century, he did so as chairman of the board of directors of Blue Bell Creameries, Inc. No longer was he manager, president, chief executive officer, secretary, or treasurer. As one who thought ahead and planned for the future, Ed had handed over day-to-day management and the title of chief executive officer to his brother Howard on April 1, 1993. Having just turned 65 and realizing he could not run the company forever, Ed still came into the office at least two days a week to work and consult. He observed with great satisfaction as the next generation began to take over and the company continued to progress in the "Blue Bell Way."

Supporting Howard in his leadership role were longstanding contributors to the company: John Barnhill remained as vice president of sales and marketing; Bill Rankin oversaw the money end of the business as chief financial officer; Gene Supak continued as vice-president of plant operations; Melvin Ziegenbein served as general sales manager; Diana Markwardt was vice-president of office operations; Paul Kruse handled the legal aspects of Blue Bell; Lyle Metzdorf steered the advertising; Ruth Goeke maintained her position as administrative assistant to Blue Bell's executives; and many excellent people hired and trained under Ed Kruse filled in the ranks.

Howard was in lockstep with Ed in following the "Blue Bell Way." That overarching idea included policies that had led Blue Bell to success, as well as those that had kept everyone headed in the same direction.

For example, the company would continue to move into new marketing areas and flourish. The cinch-by-the-inch/hard-by-the-yard plan was alive and well. Certainly, every new territory required slight tweaking, but the overall tactic served the company flawlessly.

Not only did many key employees own stock in the corporation, but also everyone received similar benefits through the employee stock option plan (ESOP). Ed described the ESOP to the employees in the company's newspaper *The Scoop* in January 1990:

> An ESOP is a type of retirement plan, similar to a profit-sharing plan. The purpose of the ESOP is to enable you to own stock in Blue Bell Creameries. Each year, if profits permit, the board of directors will authorize the company to make a contribution equal to a percentage of each covered-employee's annual earnings. This contribution will be in the form of stock or cash. If cash is contributed, it will be used to purchase stock. The plan creates a trust to do the record keeping. Your stock is held in an account administered by the trust. The dividends earned by your stock are also credited to this account. Every year, the company will hire an independent business valuation firm to determine the price of our stock. All of the stock in your account will be valued at this price. As the price changes, the value of your stock changes. When you retire, the ESOP plan will repurchase your stock at the price that exists on your retirement date. All of the contributions to the ESOP will come from Blue Bell. All of the expenses of the trust will be paid by Blue Bell. Our Employee Stock Option Plan will provide additional retirement security for you. More importantly, it will enable you to participate in the growth of the company.

A selling point Ed had always made to new recruits was that the ESOP allowed employees to work confidently without having to worry about retirement. With team members having a stake in the company's progress, the incentive for top performance remained high under Howard's leadership as well.

Blue Bell also continued to provide to employees other first-class benefits that Ed had instituted. They included medical insurance, dental insurance, life insurance, disability compensation, sick leave, a retirement plan, 401-Ks, holidays, vacations, maternity leave, and so on.

The Christmas bonus stood out as probably the most appreciated perk of all. Each year, employees received a percentage of their annual salary as a bonus. The amount directly reflected Blue Bell's profits for the year—and at peak times had reached the level of 16 percent. The Blue Bell team had plenty of motivation to make and sell the "best ice cream in the country." Ed was pleased that these incentivizing benefits continued as he handed over the reins to Howard.

In addition to promoting teamwork, the perks Ed instituted made way for camaraderie throughout the entire organization. In many companies, people just did their own thing, often performing a superb job but not really caring how other people or other departments were achieving. Blue Bell was different: A manager or department head often went out of his way to recommend promotion for an outstanding subordinate to another department, branch, or region. Even though the supervisor knew he was losing a valuable person in his own area, he realized that the company would be stronger in the long run and that the employee's efforts and talents deserved to be rewarded.

One additional advantage of everyone's having a stake in the game and caring about the performance of others and the company overall was that the working environment resisted micro-management and tended to engender more creativity. Being clear on one's responsibilities and working with others toward the goals, values, and mission of the company often fostered new ideas. This went beyond the suggestions for unique flavors of ice cream and frozen snacks. It included more efficient methods of production, ways to recycle, resolutions to needs in the community, possible tweaks to a software program, and more.

The answer to the question "What if we. . ." caused such improvements as Blue Bell's baking its own cookies instead of opening package after package of Oreos for its Cookies 'n Cream flavor. The question resulted in the backhauling of supplies and ingredients in distribution trucks after delivering ice cream to the branches. It even led to sending banana peels to a local farmer for his cows to eat, rather than dumping the peels in the landfill. These ideas and others especially thrived in an environment where the goal was to seek and accomplish what's best for the company, its customers, its consumers, its employees, and the surrounding communities.

With satisfaction, Ed also saw that his longstanding policies of treating all customers the same—with top-notch service and no pricing differentials—would continue. Throughout Ed's management of the company, grocers—and even some of Blue Bell's own salesmen—pressured Ed to give discounts to particular customers or to have special pricing in difficult markets. Ed never felt swayed by any of the arguments. All customers received the same equitable pricing and superior service from Blue Bell. *Period*. Furthermore, Ed insisted the sales force live up to commitments made to all customers and consumers. They understood the importance of this practice to Blue Bell's reputation.

Howard also followed Ed's policy of refusing to pay slotting fees to customers, contrary to the habits of most other ice cream companies. This practice amounts to buying space in the grocers' freezer cases. Blue Bell has never yielded to this demand, maintaining that the consumers should have the right to insist upon what kind of ice cream—or potato chips, soft drink, or any other commodity—they want to buy in the store. They do this through their purchases and requests to store managers. Ed knows that other ice cream businesses pass the cost of the slotting fees to their consumers. Consumers should pay for the ice cream itself, not for bribes to the grocers.

The "Blue Bell Way" of doing things worked for Ed and subsequently for Howard. The company was booming as the twenty-first century approached.

Chapter Sixteen

> Few people have original thoughts,
> so it's wise to take ideas from others
> and put them together.
>
> • EDISM #6 •

AS ED BEGAN to step back from hands-on management of Blue Bell, he had time to focus more sharply on other aspects of his life. His children were all launched into successful careers, and even grandchildren were being added to the mix. He and Evelyn had more time for travel and leisure activities. He looked for more ways to give back to the community.

Even before Ed turned over the Blue Bell reins to Howard in 1993, his family made a very sizable and important contribution to Brenham. The Kruse family had always been very active in St. Paul's Evangelical Lutheran Church, and Ed had also supported Texas Lutheran University in Seguin in many capacities, including serving on the board of regents.

One Sunday afternoon, Ed happened to attend a meeting led by Bob Green of the Lutheran Social Services of the South. Bob was there to help several well-meaning Brenham citizens discuss how to create a retirement community in the area. When the conversation ended, Ed pulled Bob aside. He told him that the eight or so people at the gathering possessed the heart but not the funds to see the project through. Ed suggested that Bob offer various aspects of the project as "naming opportunities." Furthermore, he should entice a wealthy person to make a major contribution to get the ball rolling.

Bob thanked Ed for the great suggestion and promised to consider it. Ed knew his idea was not new, but he felt it could apply perfectly to this particular situation. Ed Kruse always maintained that he'd never had an original thought, but he was pretty good at remembering and building on those of others.

Ed's plan may have outsmarted him, because two weeks later Bob Green met Ed for lunch. He presented Ed with a written proposal to name the retirement center for the Kruse family. Caught off guard, Ed said it would be a wonderful compliment to his parents to name the center the E. F. and Bertha Kruse Village, but he would have to get his siblings on board. After three months, the four surviving children of E. F. and Bertha Kruse (eldest sister Bertha Kruse Spitzer had died in 1971) decided that they could fund a large enough amount to name the village after their parents.

The siblings recruited others to take advantage of naming opportunities as well. For example, each separate living space would honor a donor; the recreation room would have a name, and many other rooms and spaces would be similarly labeled. Working together, Ed, Howard, Mildred, and Evelyn Ann raised the requisite funds, and the E. F. and Bertha Kruse Village opened in 1991, with Bertha Kruse and her four surviving children at the dedication.

Ed and Evelyn Kruse continued to support the retirement village. They later donated generous funding to create the Ewald and Hildegard Tiaden Alzheimer's Wing at Kruse Village. This area honored Evelyn's parents, and Evelyn's mother Hildegard was present at its dedication. Ed remained watchful for other possible contributions that would benefit the Brenham community.

In the meantime, he and Evelyn took time to travel. They had been to Australia and New Zealand in early 1989 with Ed's sister Mildred and her husband Charles Bridges. On that trip they kept a diary and made note of the various places the couples visited: Sydney Opera House, Norman Reef, Mossman Gorge National Park, Otway Ranges, Waitomo Glowworm Cave, Agrodome, and the Whakarewarewa Maori settlement. They also went to an orchid nursery and some dairy farms, in addition to snorkeling and attending a Rotary meeting. They even found time for some fly-fishing.

In 1998 Ed and Evelyn went on another faraway journey, this time to South Africa. On this trip, they encountered elephants, giraffes, lions, kudus, hyenas, warthogs, and many other species as they drove through Etosha National Park and Chobe National Park. They flew over Victoria Falls and took a boat cruise on the Zambezi River. In Cape Town, they visited Robben Island, where Nelson Mandela had been imprisoned. They also toured the Boschendal Plantation and stood at the lighthouse at the Cape of Good Hope.

Most of their other trips involved fishing or golf. Despite the near-fatal plane crash in 1984, Ed still loved to fish for bass at Los Mochis in Mexico, for silver salmon in Alaska—especially at Newhalen—and for speckled trout near Port O'Connor on the Texas coast. Not only did these excursions provide opportunities for Ed's favorite pastime, but they were also chances to enjoy family and friends. Another benefit was the frozen fish fillets that he brought home to prepare and eat.

Ed went on several golfing vacations. One memorable course he played was Pebble Beach in California. He also met and played with several master golfers in various pro-ams: Corey Pavin, Fred Couples, Arnold Palmer, and Lee Trevino. Ed even went to the legendary St. Andrews course in Scotland once, but he and Evelyn were on a Celtic culture trip with a group from Texas A&M, and he had no opportunity to play golf.

Ed Kruse met Arnold Palmer at a golf tournament. Courtesy of Ed. F. and Evelyn Kruse

For 15 years in a row, he and Evelyn and three other couples traveled to St. Croix in the Virgin Islands. They rented a home 1,000 feet up the side of a mountain. It was spacious and had a beautiful view of the harbor and the airport where planes came in and flew people over to St. Thomas. While the men golfed every day, the women went sightseeing, enjoyed the beaches, shopped, or just relaxed.

Golf buddies Paul LaRoche, Dr. Bob Schoenvogel, Ed Kruse, and Dr. Thomas Giddings prepare to tee off in St. Croix in the Virgin Islands. Courtesy of Ed. F. and Evelyn Kruse

One of Ed's favorite golf partners and best friends was Dr. Thomas Giddings, who also happened to be Ed's personal physician. Ed and Thomas were very competitive and possessed similar handicaps. Often the last putt determined the winner of the match. Ed took great joy in messing with Thomas over that critical putt on the 18th hole.

As Thomas prepared to swing, Ed or another of the foursome, which could include Paul LaRoche, Bob Schoenvogel, Shorty Trostle, Leroy Loesch, Gordon Parker, Pierre Roberts, or Dennis Schomburg, would "accidentally" drop his putter on the green. Thomas Giddings would step back and say, "Whenever y'all are ready, just let me know." Then he'd get back into position, and someone would cough or whisper about Thomas's mismatched socks—anything to interrupt the putter's train of thought. According to Ed, "The thing that would just really get Thomas would be for someone to say, 'You gotta have this putt, Tom, or you lose.'" Thomas would putt, white-knuckled, and more often than not miss the cup—to Ed's delight!

For some unknown reason, Thomas kept playing golf with Ed, and he and his wife were among the couples who traveled to St. Croix with the Kruses. Thomas also once diagnosed Ed with a kidney stone while they were out on the golf course. He even stopped by and gave Ed and Evelyn flu shots on his way home from the office one day each fall. Any physician who will make house calls is a close friend indeed.

Dear friends and family were indispensable to Ed and Evelyn when their oldest son, Dr. Ken Kruse, drowned tragically in the pool at his home in Houston on April 1, 1999. He was 45 years old, single, and had no children. The Kruses were devastated.

Ed did not dwell on that dark period in his life. What he would do is fondly recall Ken's mechanical and engineering prowess. For example, at one point Ken had a car in mind he wanted to buy. The Mercury Cougar had a sunroof, which Ed felt would leak like a sieve. He pointed out to Ken that no one else in Brenham owned a car with a sunroof—possibly a sign of unreliability. Ken responded that his dad had discovered his true motive. He would be the only one in Brenham *with* a sunroof. Besides, if it leaked, he would simply repair it.

Actually, it was Ken's maroon Corvette that would attract attention. One day, Ken and Lois Winkelmann (now Texas State Senator Lois Winkelmann Kolkhorst) took Ken's car out to Washington-on-the-Brazos. Ken also happened to be an expert photographer, and Lois wanted him to teach her more about the subject. While they were practicing with various angles, lenses, and shots, three men appeared and attempted to rob the pair at gunpoint. They first wanted Ken's watch, but Ken refused to give it to them since it was a gift from his parents. The bandits then took Ken's keys and drove off in his Corvette—leaving Ken and Lois stranded out in the country. The two managed to get back to Brenham, and the police later found Ken's car completely undamaged. The robbers had merely taken it for a joyride.

One afternoon Ed walked out to the garage and Ken had all the wires out of the console. According to Ed, "It looked like an electrician's nightmare!" Ed further marveled when Ken "wired it all up so that before you could start the car, you had three different buttons you had to press in sequence. If you didn't push those three buttons, you could drive one mile, and the carburetor would shut off. You couldn't go any farther. So if anybody ever stole the car again, they'd never get anywhere."

Ken's mechanical expertise was further demonstrated when he installed a sprinkler system in the yard of his brother Neil. There just didn't seem to be anything that Ken couldn't do with his hands. This included work done on Ken's own home in Houston. The house, near Houston's medical center, was a labor of love to Ken. That it contributed to his death seems terribly ironic.

It did not make sense to Ed why someone with Ken's intelligence, skill, worth, and potential would be snatched away at such a young age. Not understanding God's reasoning, Ed tried to keep moving in a positive direction—one step at a time. Giving back to his community helped him ease his grief.

For example, he encouraged Blue Bell and its shareholders to contribute to a swimming center to be located just down the road from the company headquarters and to be run by the City of Brenham. Completed in 2001, the Blue Bell Aquatic Center features three pools. The outside leisure pool has water slides, spray hoses, and other equipment for play. Inside the building is a six-lane competition pool for swim team practice, lap drills, and water safety instruction. The third pool is heated for physical therapy purposes. Ed was proud that the center serves people of all ages and needs.

Ed was also instrumental in the development of Hohlt Park, which was dedicated in May 2002. This project was a joint venture of the City of Brenham, Washington County, Blinn College, and several other local entities. With the park itself and separate fields reflecting the contributions made by individuals through naming opportunities, Hohlt Park covers 85 acres. It features eight baseball/softball fields with bleachers and scoreboards, eleven soccer fields, three sand volleyball courts, nine holes of disc golf, a mile-long jogging/walking path, playscapes, an all-sports building, and the Dr. Bobbie M. Dietrich Memorial Amphitheater. Hohlt Park, named for longtime Blue Bell president Herbert Hohlt and his wife Letha, along with Fireman's Park and other outdoor facilities, have made Brenham a mecca for youth sports tournaments. Ed liked the fact that visitors were drawn to Brenham for such wholesome activities.

Ed's contributions to the community did not go unnoticed. As far back as 1987, Washington County recognized him as the Man of the Year. In 1995 Lutheran Social Services of the South named him Lutheran of the Year. In 2001 Ed received an honorary degree—Doctor of Humane Letters, Honoris Causa—from Texas Lutheran University. He and Evelyn were also acknowledged publicly for their many generous scholarships to Texas A&M University.

Ed was proud of the fact that his daughter Karen also contributed to the world around her. In 2003 Karen received the Angels in Adoption Award from the Congressional Committee on Adoption for her work in aiding orphans from Kazakhstan. Over the years, Karen and her husband Wes Hall have adopted thirteen children—from Russia, the Philippines, and Uganda. That total does not include the four children and three children the couple brought into their marriage, respectively. In addition, Karen and Wes have been responsible, directly or indirectly, for finding homes for over 700 other orphans.

Karen is the founder and president of Central Texas Orphan Mission Alliance (CTOMA). Its goal is "to help meet the physical, medical, and spiritual needs of orphans in the U.S. and abroad." One of the ways CTOMA reaches its objectives is through starting new orphan ministries in Christian churches. According to the organization's website (www. ctoma.org), the foundation's efforts are "currently focused in Uganda, Mexico, and Central America." The group also works closely with missionaries in the Bryan/College Station area and in Belton, Texas.

All CTOMA donations go directly to orphan ministries; the organization has no paid employees. Even the doctors and nurses who travel to remote areas receive no remuneration whatsoever—in fact, they pay their own travel expenses. In addition, CTOMA drills water wells, opens schools, and provides medical supplies and training in missions. It even helps during local disasters such as hurricanes, floods, and tornadoes.

Karen has been known to stand up to corrupt foreign officials who wanted to confiscate her boxes of medications and medical supplies destined for orphans in need. The border patrols would much prefer to sell them for their own personal gain or use them to supply armies. Unrelenting, Karen gets her way. Ed admired her pluck and energy and sometimes wondered if she's half crazy for the problems and responsibilities she undertakes. But there was a twinkle of pride in his eyes as he groused.

The same year that Karen received her recognition from Congress, the Kruses were hit again with unimaginable tragedy: On August 11, 2003, their youngest child Dr. Neil Kruse succumbed to inoperable cancer. Like his brother Ken, Neil was only 45 years old when he died.

Did knowing that Neil's case was terminal and praying for an end to his suffering make his death any easier than Ken's? Not in the least. Living across the country from Neil's home in South Carolina and unable to give constant hands-on comfort and care to Neil and his family probably contributed to Ed's and Evelyn's hopelessness. Ed even decided to build a new house to distract them from Neil's illness. Nothing helped.

In 1996 Neil, his wife Janie, and their two children Jordan and Claire had closed Neil's 12-year-old dental practice in Brenham and moved to Mount Pleasant, South Carolina. As a first grader, Jordan had been diagnosed with profound dyslexia and ADHD, and his parents sought the very best school for him to address his needs. They turned to Trident Academy in Mount Pleasant for "bright children who learn differently."

Neil and Janie supported the school in every way possible. In the meantime, they began to develop real estate—converting the old Charleston County jail into an office building, constructing a high-rise boat facility next door, and developing property next to Lake Keowee. Just as he had been an excellent dentist, Neil proved to be an insightful developer—able to visualize potential opportunities and turn them into reality.

After Neil died, Ed wrote to Jordan and Claire about their father. He was afraid that their memories of what a special person Neil was might fade over the years. After all, Jordan was only 15 and Claire 12 when their father passed away. In his letter, Ed mentioned what an accomplished swimmer, springboard diver, SCUBA diver, and trampolinist their dad was. He referred to Neil's interests in hunting and taxidermy, the latter skill he learned from Evelyn's uncle, Johnny Tiaden.

Neil's strong character came into play in an incident Ed related to Jordan and Claire. In dental school, Neil was required to find a patient whose teeth needed extensive work and who would agree to have him fix her problems. A recent immigrant volunteered, but she was terribly frightened. Neil promised the woman he would be gentle. Everything was going according to the plan until one of his professors checked Neil's work and was displeased at the *rate* it was progressing. The superior took over and began cutting away on the woman's gums in a very rough manner. Neil was appalled and reported the instructor to the dean of the Dental School. He stood up for what was right, even though he could have been disciplined for going over the professor's head. Neil practiced what all the Kruses had been taught—"No one ever gets lost on a straight road."

Ed also wanted Neil's children to know that others recognized their dad's tender nature. When he graduated from dental school, Neil was given the "heart" award for being the dentist the hygienists would most like to take home.

Ed's letter to Neil's children came straight from his heart. There is no question that they would always have a true sense of their dad, his outstanding qualities and accomplishments, and his everlasting love for them and their mom.

Ed encouraged Janie to remarry when the right man came along. Several years later, Tony, who had lost his wife to cancer, respectfully approached Janie's parents, as well as Ed and Evelyn, before he asked Janie to marry him. Ed and Evelyn were delighted with the match and remained close to Janie, Jordan, Claire, Tony, and Tony's three children.

An announcement late in 2003 brought some light back into Ed Kruse's life. After a very productive and successful career, Howard Kruse decided that he would retire on the 50th anniversary of his return to Blue Bell as a full-time employee. That date would be May 1, 2004. As his brother had done before him, Howard wanted to prepare the company for the change in leadership. Therefore, six months before his retirement, he recommended that Paul W. Kruse, Ed's son and legal counsel at Blue Bell, be named president and chief executive officer of Blue Bell Creameries as of May 1, 2004. The board of directors unanimously gave its stamp of approval in December 2003, and the company readied for a seamless passing of the torch.

Chapter Seventeen

If you can do some good, do it now.

• EDISM #24 •

ONE CAN ONLY IMAGINE Ed's pride on May 1, 2004, as Paul W. Kruse became the third generation of the family to lead Blue Bell. Paul, almost 50 years old, married to Barbara "Babs" McMartin from Beaman, Iowa, and the father of Audra, Wes, and Gwen, had now been with the company full-time for almost 20 years. He had played a major role in Blue Bell's continuing success. His sharp legal mind, ease at taking on challenges, and ability to find solutions prepared him well for his new responsibilities. With Ed as chairman of the board and Howard serving as president emeritus, Paul had two seasoned leaders to help him. Often, they were literally only steps away, because Ed and Howard still worked in their offices more days than not.

Even though some of the extremely valuable veterans were beginning to retire—John Barnhill, Melvin Ziegenbein, and Eugene Supak, Ed had been instrumental in hiring the men who would eventually take their places and had confidence in their capacities as leaders in the company. During the next 10 years, Ricky Dickson became vice-president of sales and marketing, Greg Bridges took over the reins of plant operations, and Wayne Hugo rose to the position of general sales manager.

Ricky Dickson, a Baylor University graduate, is sharp, enthusiastic, energetic, and unflappable. Even though he rose up through the sales ranks, his people skills and his capacity to take on challenges were such that Howard actually placed him in charge of the Broken Arrow plant at one point when new management was needed. He performed outstandingly. When Melvin Ziegenbein became vice president of sales and marketing, Ricky succeeded him as general sales manager. Upon Melvin's retirement, Ricky rose to the position of vice president of sales and marketing.

Ed's son Paul W. Kruse is now CEO and president of Blue Bell Creameries. Courtesy of Blue Bell Creameries

Greg Bridges, the son of Ed and Howard's sister Mildred, attended Texas A&M and graduated with a degree in dairy science. He joined Blue Bell full-time in 1985 and worked intently in the plant under Howard Kruse and Gene Supak. His quick intelligence, industriousness, attention to detail, and innumerable other abilities helped him succeed. Quiet and serious, he has an understated sense of humor that catches one by surprise. Ed remarked, "I'd be proud to have Greg as a son"—high praise indeed. When Gene Supak retired, Greg became vice president of plant operations.

Wayne Hugo was born in Brenham but grew up in Houston. After graduating from Smiley High School, he attended San Jacinto College for a while and spent two years in the US Army. Answering a Blue Bell ad in 1974, Wayne was hired as a driver-salesman in Houston, became a route supervisor in 1977, and ascended to territory manager in the Westheimer area of Houston in 1981. He continued to move up through the company—becoming the branch manager in Mobile, Alabama, in 1993 and regional manager in 2005. Wayne came full circle when he returned to Brenham to take Ricky Dickson's place as general sales manager. Wayne epitomizes the capacity of any Blue Bell employee to rise all the way to the top by enhancing his considerable aptitude with uncompromising positive attitude.

Paul Kruse has had a great team to support his own substantial abilities. Like his dad, Paul is very personable, and the two share many other valuable traits. For example, both were studiously aware of the talents and capabilities of the people around them and trusted them to receive a project and run with it. Ed and Paul were affable and disarming in conferring with buyers or customers, yet they stood their ground if push came to shove. They both possessed superior judgment of character and displayed the ethical standards that would make E. F. very pleased. Like his dad, Paul feels heavily his responsibilities to employees, customers, consumers, buyers, and stockholders.

One additional characteristic the two men had in common is a sense of humor. Whereas Ed always had a joke to tell, Paul is more of a tease. A typical example was the day that Paul was leaving the office for lunch and there was a huge group of children waiting to get off their school bus to take a tour of the creamery. Paul went to the side of the bus and talked to the children who were looking through the windows. He told them, "Don't get off. You'll have to come back another day." The children asked, "Why?" Paul replied, "We ate all we could! There's no ice cream left!" The children took Paul seriously for about a split second; then they started laughing.

When Blue Bell made the decision in 2010 to reroute the tour of the creamery, enlarge the visitor's center, and create a larger parlor and gift shop, Paul studied the committee's plan carefully and approved it, with one exception: He suggested the addition of an area where

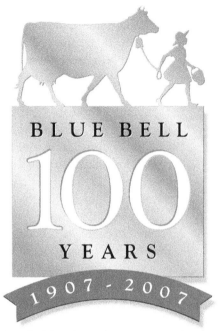

Blue Bell celebrated its 100th anniversary in 2007. Courtesy of Blue Bell Creameries

visitors could feel the –20 degrees Fahrenheit temperature of the cold storage unit. Remembering the appeal of that frigid chamber when he was a child, Paul wanted visitors to experience it firsthand.

Paul works very hard at his job and obviously loves what he does. Not only did the company celebrate its 100th anniversary in 2007 under Paul's watch, but its sales territory continued to expand the "Blue Bell Way."

With Paul handling the Blue Bell responsibilities, Ed devoted much time to figuring out additional ways to enhance the conditions of communities around him. He recently targeted Texas A&M University, Brenham High School, Blinn College, and the City of Brenham.

Ed said he owes a deep debt of gratitude to Texas A&M. Not only did he and his brother receive excellent educations, discipline, and preparation for life while students there, but so did his four children, some of his grandchildren, and many of the outstanding employees of Blue Bell Creameries. Besides, Ed loved all sports and had a special place in his heart for the Aggies.

For these reasons, the College of Agriculture, the 12th Man Foundation, and the athletics department have all benefited from the Kruses' largesse in the way of scholarships and cash donations. Ed also spearheaded a large gift from Howard, Blue Bell Creameries, and himself when they donated $7 million to rename and renovate the baseball facilities at Texas A&M. The complex is now known as Olsen Field at Blue Bell Park. According to the Aggie baseball team, they have the "sweetest facility in all of college baseball."

In return, Texas A&M University has bestowed honors on Ed. Among the many ways Texas A&M has recognized him include the Texas A&M College of Agriculture and Life Sciences Outstanding Alumni Award (2002), induction into the Texas A&M Corps of Cadets Hall of Honor (2003), and the first Lifetime Achievement Award from the Letterman's Association (2012).

The award Ed Kruse most treasured, however, is the Texas A&M University Distinguished Alumnus Award, presented in 2005. Ed's video on the Wall of Tribute page at the Texas A&M website tells of his countless contributions to the university and reveals some of the advantages he felt he gained from being in the Corps of Cadets. Those include straight talk, strict discipline, and taking responsibility for one's actions. No excuses. *Period.* The video also praises Ed for the simple tenets he strives to live by and advises others to follow:

> Be honest.
> Be sincere.
> Work hard.
> Look people in the eye.
> Tell them the truth.

Although Ed never sought recognition for his donations, sometimes it came in very unexpected ways. One day when Ed was fishing in Port O'Connor, he and Kelly Parks, his guide of 25 years, pulled aside Robert "Froggy" Sanders' shrimp boat and asked if Froggy could save him about 40 pounds of shrimp to take back to Brenham. Froggy had grown up in Port Lavaca and played backup at Texas A&M to Heisman Trophy halfback John David Crow.

Responding to Ed's request, Froggy said he'd see what he could do. When Ed finished fishing, Froggy had the shrimp ready and put them in the car for him. Then he refused to let Ed pay for the shrimp. He said, "You don't owe me a thing. I appreciate what you've done for A&M and the baseball stadium." Truly touched by Froggy's generosity and thoughtful words, Ed accepted the gift graciously.

One of Ed Kruse's proudest moments was receiving the Distinguished Alumnus Award from Texas A&M University in 2005. Courtesy of Ed. F. and Evelyn Kruse

As much as Ed was grateful to Texas A&M for bettering his life, he supported Brenham High School for many of the same reasons. The school's academics, athletics, extracurricular activities, and life lessons are superior. Ed felt very fortunate that he, his children, and many Blue Bell employees grew up in a community where excellence in education is stressed and standards are high.

Ed religiously followed the Brenham High School Honor Rolls that were published in the *Brenham Banner-Press*. He attended many sporting events—including football, volleyball, soccer, basketball, baseball, softball, and track. He and Evelyn went to BHS musical performances and plays. Ed was very much aware of outstanding students and contributed to scholarships that provided them a leg-up as they went through college. If a teacher or coach perceived a need for a student, he or she would sometimes contact the Kruses for help. "You bet!" was always the response.

Ed particularly admired BHS athletic director Glen West, a superb role model for the high school students. Glen worked hard at his job—often up past midnight designing programs and scouting opponents. He absolutely followed the straight and narrow and expected his players to do likewise. If a student was not willing to adhere to the policies (like no piercings or tattoos), he or she did not participate in sports at BHS. On the other hand,

Glen would go the extra mile to counsel and help kids. He's like a father to many of the athletes.

One Glen West story epitomizes Edism #25—"Be prepared." It seems that Glen had a second-string quarterback on his team by the name of Michael Buro. Although he seldom received an opportunity to play, Buro was always at the ready. In a state quarterfinal game, the Brenham starting quarterback was injured by a vicious tackle and had to leave the game. Buro was sent in with a play. He passed perfectly to his wide receiver for a touchdown. In the state final two weeks later, the quarterback got sacked again and left the game. Buro went in with only the fourth down remaining and proceeded to connect again on a touchdown pass. Two plays only—two different games, two touchdowns: the essence of preparedness.

In 2007 the Ed and Howard Kruse Field House at Brenham High School opened. It was made possible by contributions and fundraising efforts initiated by the Kruse brothers and Blue Bell Creameries. The facility promotes weight training by all athletes and features dressing rooms for teams participating in outdoor sports. The Kruses and Blue Bell further supported the Cubs' athletic programs through advertising at their football stadium, baseball field, and other venues.

One of Ed's greatest honors was being named a Distinguished Alumnus of Brenham High School in 2004. His induction into the Brenham Cubs Hall of Fame two years later also pleased Ed greatly. The inscription on his plaque reads:

> Ed Kruse was a standout quarterback for the Brenham Cubs. Under his leadership, the 1944 Cubs went 8–2 before losing to El Campo in bi-district. While there were no all-star teams picked during the latter years of World War II, Kruse was described by his coach Owen Erekson "as one of the best all-around quarterbacks in Class A circles in Texas." Senior year 1944, Kruse played defensive secondary as well as quarterback. During that campaign, he also had a 55% completion ratio passing. Following graduation, Kruse continued to support the Cubs and has remained a loyal fan and strong supporter of Brenham Schools and athletic programs. As chief executive with Blue Bell Creameries, he applied virtues learned. Blue Bell has become one of the largest ice cream producers in the U.S.

Blinn College was also on Ed's radar screen. The Kruses supported and endowed many scholarships over the years. In addition, Ed led the fundraising to establish the W. J. "Bill" Rankin Agricultural Complex on the Brenham Blinn campus in 2010. In 2013 the surviving children of E. F. and

Bertha Kruse and their spouses contributed a significant gift to Blinn for the Kruse Center, a new recreational, activity, and athletic facility on the Blinn College-Brenham campus.

In December 2013, Ed and Evelyn Kruse donated 100 acres in south Brenham off Highway 290 for the Brenham Family Park for the enjoyment of all the residents of Washington County and its visitors. The master plan has yet to be drawn, but there will be a 6- to 7-acre lake, located on Woodward Creek, as a focal point. Ed spent years finding the right property and working with governmental entities to see what would best suit their needs. He enjoyed donating to the nurturing community where he had the privilege to grow up and raise his children.

Giving was pure pleasure to Ed. He truly believed John Bunyan's advice, "He who bestows his goods upon the poor, shall have as much again and ten times more." He even found research to back up the fact that those who give more actually end up earning more. But that's not the reason he was so philanthropic. He had the means, he saw the need, and he could directly effect positive change in peoples' lives. It was a win/win situation for all concerned.

Full of excess energy, Ed also thrived on devising opportunities for his huge family to get together. Ed and Evelyn have twenty-two grandchildren: Karen has seventeen children, Paul has three, and Neil's two children remain as close to the family as always. At the end of 2014, there were a total of three great-grandchildren. There is a prayer in Psalm 128:6 that reads, "May you live to see your children's children." Ed's and Evelyn's blessings abounded.

Many of Ed's plans revolved around holidays—bringing the family together in one place for Thanksgiving, Christmas, or the Fourth of July. Often these events took place at Ed and Evelyn's home, but sometimes Ed arranged destination reunions. In recent years, the Kruses met at a dude ranch in Bandera, Texas, at a resort in Grapevine, Texas, and at a retreat in Hilton Head, South Carolina.

Once considered too tame a way for him to travel, Ed scheduled cruises for the family. The Kruses have voyaged to Cozumel and to Alaska. As with resorts, the cruises allow participants to unpack and stay in one place. The boat does the traveling, and the crew provides the meals and entertainment. It's easy and enjoyable for everyone.

Sometimes Ed would take smaller groups on excursions. He gathered several of his granddaughters for salmon and halibut fishing in Alaska and a few of his grandsons for mule deer hunting in West Texas. He was always ready to round up family members for a quick fishing trip to the Texas

Gulf Coast or for duck hunting in South Texas. As with his own children, Ed was still hopeful that the grandchildren would catch or bag the limit. His competitive spirit remained fully intact—that is, until it came to dove hunting: Once Ed learned that doves mate for life, he lost interest in the sport. Even though Ed hunted for food and made sure all of his catch was eaten, something bothered him about depriving a dove of its lifelong partner.

One of Ed's famous sayings to the kids and grandkids was, "Put all the lead in the duck." In other words, if you're going to shoot the duck, aim your shotgun well before you pull the trigger. Make sure you bring it down. Applied to life, it means: "If you've got a goal, go for it all the way."

Ed discovered that it was much easier to be a grandparent than a parent. One was not responsible for making sure the homework is done, the sports practice is run correctly, the squabbles are quashed, the goals are met, the curfews are adhered to, or the discipline is accomplished. Granddad enjoyed being on the sidelines and cheering everyone on.

Looking back at his life when his children were growing up, Ed would probably say that he spent less time with Evelyn and the children than he wanted, he may have been somewhat distracted about work problems when he was with them, he was probably too strict, he might have been too intense in pushing them to meet goals, and he definitely should have given more hugs and more praise. Given a second chance with his grandchildren, he made up for lost time.

Some of Ed's most poignant moments with his adopted granddaughters were accompanying them down the aisle of their church to be married. When they arrived at the altar, not only was the bridegroom waiting, but so was their father, Wes Hall, a former judge, who conducted the ceremony. Walking back to join Evelyn in their pew, Ed looked out to see the loving family, friends, and colleagues who had so blessed his life. He felt totally fulfilled.

Chapter Eighteen

Thank people who have helped you.

• EDISM #21 •

LIKE A WEDDING BAND, Ed and Evelyn Kruse came full circle. They were the only two living at home. Their marriage was stronger than ever. Ed loved Evelyn more every day.

The couple had weathered many storms and shared many celebrations. Their most painful times, of course, were the heartbreaking deaths of their sons Ken and Neil. Whereas such tragedies often pull families apart, these grief-filled periods drew Ed and Evelyn closer.

The two of them also experienced the ups and downs of Blue Bell as one. After the first few hectic, work-around-the-clock years of struggling to master the duties of manager, Ed arrived home each evening at precisely 5:05 p.m. Evelyn, preparing dinner, could see him from the kitchen window as he stopped at the mailbox to pick up the mail. She could tell from his posture what kind of day he'd had. They would discuss the details later, because spending time with the children at dinner and during their evening activities took priority. But after the children went to bed, Ed revealed what was happening at the office. Evelyn was there to listen, commiserate, comfort, advise, encourage, and applaud.

Together they faced scares and illnesses: Ed's airplane crash in 1984 comes to mind. Then there was the telephone call Ed received on October 30, 2006. After the usual banter, his physician revealed the dreaded news: "Ed, the biopsy shows malignant cells in your left ureter. We won't truly know the extent of your cancer until you undergo surgery. It may have spread to your kidney and elsewhere. More testing needs to be done. I'm going to refer you to M. D. Anderson Cancer Center in Houston."

Between the startling diagnosis and the actual surgery on November 9,

Ed and Evelyn Kruse enjoy a successful fishing trip with some of their granddaughters in Alaska. Courtesy of Ed. F. and Evelyn Kruse

2006, there were several very tense days. Ed's thoughts constantly switched from Neil's courageous battle, to his father's death at age 56 following surgery for stomach cancer, to his own mortality. After all, he was 78 years old.

Fortunately, the best of all possible scenarios occurred. The tumor was strictly confined to the left ureter, the tube that runs from the left kidney to the bladder. Since Ed's healthy right kidney was functioning well, the surgeon removed the cancerous ureter, along with Ed's malformed left kidney. There were no malignant cells left in the area. Additional tests showed that all lymph nodes were cancer-free, as were his major organs. This meant that Ed would require neither chemotherapy nor radiation and that he should be just fine with his strong right kidney to do all the work. Once he recovered from the surgery, he mainly needed check-ups at M. D. Anderson to be sure there was no recurrence. He had dodged yet another bullet.

In 2012 Ed was diagnosed with Type II diabetes, despite his slight frame and healthy lifestyle. Oral medication kept his glucose levels in the desired range. He also had several skin lesions removed from his face—all those hours of fishing and playing golf in the sun took their toll. In 2013 Ed had back surgery to relieve severe nerve pain. Evelyn had her own issues—neuropathy in her feet and hypertension, the latter of which daughter Karen teased was a result of putting up with her dad!

To boost Karen's claim is the incident in which Evelyn was driving too fast and got pulled over by a policeman. The officer approached the car and said, "Lady, you were going a little fast there." Before Evelyn could say anything, Ed spoke up, "Yes, sir, she was! I've been trying to tell her! With her, it's just put the pedal to the metal! Here we go! Go! Go! Go! I've been telling her all along! You're going to get a ticket! But do you think she's going to listen to me? Oh, no! There she goes! Going! Going! Going! I've been telling her! What can you do? You can only tell 'em so much! And they just don't listen to you!"

Ed, who had an anathema to speeding tickets and had talked himself out of several, kept up the rant for as long as he could think of something to say. Finally, the patrolman shook his head and said to her, "Lady, you need to slow down," and walked back to his car. Evelyn glared at Ed and muttered, "Have you gone crazy?" He replied, "You didn't get a ticket, did you? I did the job for him. I chewed you out. He felt sorry for you and didn't have to ticket you." Evelyn probably would have preferred the ticket. . . .

For the most part, their medical conditions were just bumps in the road. Ed figured if one lives long enough, defects and breakdowns are bound to occur. His philosophy was to follow his doctor's orders—take the pills, get the X-ray, undergo the procedure, do the physical therapy, and follow the prescribed regimen. As a precaution, Ed plugged in his and Evelyn's cell phones each night—to be sure the batteries were fully charged in case a problem arose when they were away from home separately.

And they kept busy schedules—Evelyn was hands-on with the grand-children, had duties at church, drove to College Station to help Karen with projects, and enjoyed flower-arranging opportunities with friends. Ed stopped by the office to check in and make the rounds, met with various people concerning fundraising projects, and attended Rotary Club. He was a regular at meetings at the George H. W. Bush School of Government and Public Service at Texas A&M, and he delighted in Brenham High School sporting events.

Ed was probably out and about more than Evelyn. He was very much a people person. He looked for excuses to go to the grocery store. These trips helped Evelyn and gave Ed a chance to check out the ice cream sec-tion. However, he also took the opportunity—and the pleasure—to strike up conversations with other shoppers about food choices, sports, family, and anything else.

Ed knew it embarrassed Evelyn, their children, and their grandchildren when he talked to anyone and everyone. From restaurant servers to US presidents, Ed simply enjoyed conversing with people and learning what made them tick. He knew no strangers.

Even doctor's visits could be fun. If there were a friend or acquaintance in the waiting room, they gave updates on their lives and Ed would tell a joke or two. He brought other patients into the conversation, and it could become a relaxed scene. No one fretted if the doctor was behind schedule when Ed was entertaining in the waiting room!

At home, Ed admitted that he was somewhat hyper. He definitely had a plan when he got up each morning. He might study information about particular stocks or bonds that had been recommended—or possibly other investments concerning land or mineral interests. He might review his annual balance statement, which he did by hand. Tracking where money came from, determining where it was spent, and judging whether he got the proper bang for each buck could be on the day's agenda. He went through the mail and paid bills. He picked up the phone to catch up with friends—no email or text messaging for Ed Kruse.

However, the process that probably took up the majority of Ed's desk time was assessing whether his resources were allocated in positive, productive, and helpful ways. He was always looking for worthy causes to support.

When he could not sit any longer, Ed took Molly, the Kruses' pudgy dachshund-chow mix, for a 30-minute walk on the 75 acres surrounding their home. That exercise also gave him an opportunity to check on his property and visit with a neighbor or two.

Ed and Evelyn Kruse celebrated 65 years of marriage, children, Blue Bell, and Brenham on June 18, 2015. Courtesy of Ed. F. and Evelyn Kruse

Ed was somewhat fanatical about his weight—stepping on the scale twice a day. The only time he worried was if the reading was three pounds over his normal weight for a few days in a row. At that point, he would cut down on calories until he reached the desired number again. Three pounds were easier to lose than ten.

Ed ate moderate servings of a wide variety of foods. He didn't cook much, with the exception of sautéing or grilling fish, but he often played sous-chef to Evelyn. They entertained guests occasionally just to visit, or to play 42 or bridge, or for Aggie football weekends. The couple watched television together—generally sports. Evelyn, particularly, enjoyed the big tennis tournaments—Wimbledon and the US Open, for example.

The two of them read books and newspapers. They were mentally sharp and in good physical shape for people in their mid-80s. Both Ed and Evelyn could probably look forward to many quality years ahead: Ed's mother Bertha lived to be almost 99; his sister Mildred is 92 and hasn't missed a beat; Evelyn's mother Hildegard was 104 when she passed away.

It was gratifying for Ed and Evelyn to look back on their life together. They felt it had been a true honor to be involved with all the people at Blue Bell over so many years and to watch each person's contributions toward the growth and success of the company.

When the couple reviewed their children's meaningful lives, they were very pleased. To have all four in professions was a tribute to the hard work and dedication put forth by each child, as well as the efforts of their instructors and mentors. Even in their short lives, Ken and Neil provided effective, painless treatments for their dental patients. They both enhanced the beauty of their surroundings and positively influenced the people around them, including friends, acquaintances, and family.

Paul relishes his job at the helm of Blue Bell Creameries. Meanwhile, he contributes immeasurably to the dairy industry through his leadership in several statewide, national, and international organizations. He also devotes much energy to the Brenham community through his active participation in Boy Scouts, Texas 4-H, Blinn College, and many other associations. An exemplary husband and father, Paul lives up to every expectation his parents could have for their son.

To observe Karen keeping up with her large family, missionary work, the farm, her artistic endeavors, and more left Ed and Evelyn breathless. Ed wondered why he and Evelyn never thought to adopt children. His daughter inspired him.

The Kruses' grandchildren are completing fine records—in academics, athletics, and extracurricular activities—in high school, college, and graduate school. They are beginning to launch themselves successfully into the adult world. In the meantime, they're reflecting well on their parents and their grandparents, who love them dearly.

Over the years, Ed and Evelyn treasured close friendships. They traveled the world. They spent time with US presidents, well-known sports figures, and famous entertainers. They had the opportunity to give back to their community and to say "thank you" for the quality of their lives.

Ed Kruse would never take an ounce of credit for any of the blessings. He would point to God, family, the folks at Blue Bell, coaches, teachers,

Barbara Bush, President George H. W. Bush, Evelyn Kruse, and Ed. F. Kruse. Courtesy of Ed. F. and Evelyn Kruse

and other helpful, intriguing role models he and Evelyn encountered along life's path.

And he would pull out his list of thirty-three Edisms and indicate their influence in helping him stay on track.

For instance, time and time again, Ed Kruse overcame challenges by working hard enough and long enough (Edism #5). The prime example was taking on the responsibility of managing Blue Bell Creameries at the age of 23. There was so much to do, so much to learn, so many problems to solve, and so many people depending on him to rise to the occasion. Ed's intelligence, education, and experience, along with trusted mentors, played major roles, but it was the countless hours of arduous work that helped him succeed during those first uncertain years at the Blue Bell helm.

Finding funding for the new plant in 1971 after the Houston bank backed out, restoring the plant to safe working conditions after the ammonia leak in 1973, pitching in to help provide product to those grocers who took the risk to put Blue Bell on special in the early Houston days, and many other important and meaningful endeavors in his life have been achievable because Ed remembered that hard work could compensate for other shortcomings. Not surprisingly, the harder Ed worked, the luckier he got (Edism #18).

Two other principles also served Ed well time and time again. Whether he was debating a military career versus one in the dairy industry, contemplating the best car to buy, or readying Blue Bell for its future as he eased away from the leadership role, Ed thought ahead (Edism #32) and became prepared (Edism #25).

In certain situations, these two important habits became intertwined with another: "It's a cinch by the inch, hard by the yard" (Edism #11). This combination is particularly seen in the methods Ed employed to grow Blue Bell's sales territory. He set his sights on major population areas contiguous to current sales regions. He made sure grocers wanted Blue Bell to enter the new market and ensured that he had trained personnel who could staff it. He coordinated sales with production by verifying that the plant had the capacity to provide the additional product under strict quality control and delivery by the Blue Bell team. Only when these criteria were met did Ed approve entry into a new sales area. The practice worked successfully for Blue Bell.

Some of Ed's principles reflect his philanthropy. The community of Brenham, along with many other entities, benefited because of the Kruses' generosity: "It's good to be benevolent" (Edism #9). But without sacrificing and reinvesting their own money back into Blue Bell Creameries, the Kruses might not have had the means to support laudable organizations: "Be strong enough to delay gratification" (Edism #28). By encouraging others to donate to worthy causes and to delight in the positive impact of their contributions on the communities served, Ed provided an opportunity for many to recognize that "It's more blessed to give than to receive" (Edism #12) .

As these examples demonstrate, Ed's reliance on his basic principles permeated every portion of his life's story. It would have been simple, though highly disruptive, to place an Edism reference after practically every paragraph in this account. The following snippets establish that point:

1. There is no question that Ed and Evelyn Kruse had a long, successful marriage—despite tragedies and overwhelming pressures. Deep love and abiding respect held them together and brought them closer, but so did their devotion to their wedding vows: "Do what you say you're going to do" (Edism #26). Having the perseverance to stick together through the rough times often makes a relationship even stronger.
2. When Ed confessed to his children that the $20 he had gambled in a Las Vegas casino had, in fact, become $60, he was "being honest in all his dealings" (Edism #22).

3. Hiring women to work in the plant in the early 1950s wasn't an original thought, but it was a progressive and beneficial step for Blue Bell Creameries: "Few people have original thoughts, so it's wise to take ideas from others and put them together" (Edism #6).
4. Vendors who took advantage of Ed's youth and crooks who stole from the company during his early days of managing Blue Bell quickly learned that "integrity is not negotiable" (Edism #3).
5. Ed took pride in every job that he undertook in his life—from paring peaches, to scrubbing ice cream cans, to edging his parents' sidewalk with a hoe, to putting up with the jealous salesmen at Swift and Co. He always did "a common job uncommonly well" (Edism #31).
6. Even Ed's mild obsession about maintaining his weight brings certain principles to mind: "Moderation [in eating, drinking, exercising, etc.] is the key" (Edism #10). It's also easier to lose three pounds than it is ten: "It's a cinch by the inch, hard by the yard" (Edism #11).

Obviously, intertwining Edisms with Ed's life story can reach the point of absurdity, but the weight example indicates the extent to which the principles were ingrained in Ed's being. Ed's thought was that one of the "good" reasons God had him on Earth (Edism #8) was so he could pass along these thirty-three nuggets of wisdom and demonstrate their benefits to his own journey.

Ed didn't give himself credit for following these principles. Throughout his life, he merely took the next step along a straight road. He didn't get lost (Edism #1).

Maybe it's time to add another Edism to the list.

#34. It's good to be humble.

Ed Kruse was a good and humble man. *Period*.

> It's good to be humble.
>
> • EDISM #34 •

ED. F. KRUSE died on Wednesday, September 23, 2015, shortly before this book went to print. God must have finally decided that there was no more left for him to do. (Edism #8)

Below is Ed's obituary. According to his wishes, it is simple and to the point:

Edward Fred Kruse, 87, husband of Evelyn Tiaden Kruse, died Sept. 23, 2015 in College Station.

Funeral services are scheduled for 2:00 p.m., Saturday, Sept. 26, 2015 at the Brenham High School auditorium, with Pastor Phil Fenton officiating. A private family burial at Prairie Lea Cemetery will follow later in the afternoon. Visitation will be from 5:00 to 8:30 p.m. Friday evening at Memorial Oaks Chapel.

Mr. Kruse was born March 15, 1928 in Brenham to Eddie Fritz and Bertha Quebe Kruse. He was married to Evelyn Tiaden on June 18, 1950 at St. Paul's Evangelical Lutheran Church. He continued membership there until his death. Mr. Kruse was the retired CEO and Chairman of the Board of Blue Bell Creameries.

Survivors include his wife, Evelyn Kruse of Brenham; son and daughter-in-law Paul and Barbara Kruse of Brenham; daughter and son-in-law Karen and Wes Hall of College Station; daughter-in-law Jane Skatell of Charleston, S.C.; brother and sister-in-law Howard and Verlin Kruse of Brenham; sisters Evelyn Ann Kruse and Mildred Bridges, also of Brenham. Also surviving are numerous grandchildren and great-grandchildren.

He was preceded in death by his parents and two sons, Ken Kruse and Neil Kruse.

Serving as pallbearers are grandsons Wes Kruse, Michael Bosse, Jason Potts, Chris Kee, Emmanuel Hall, and Jordan Kruse.

Memorials in Mr. Kruse's memory may be directed to St. Paul's Christian Day School, 305 W. Third St., Brenham, Texas, 77833; Central Texas Orphan Mission Alliance (CTOMA), 4100 E. 29th St. Bryan, Texas 77802, or to a favorite charity.

Funeral arrangements for Edward Fred Kruse are entrusted to Memorial Oaks Chapel, 1306 West Main, Brenham. To post a tribute to the family, visit www.memorialoakschapel.com.

Reflecting his faith, the tune chosen for moving Ed's casket into the funeral service was a child's first hymn, "Jesus Loves Me, This I Know." Again, simple and to the point.

Ed. F. Kruse is deeply missed by his family, his friends, the folks at Blue Bell Creameries, the Brenham community, the Aggies of Texas A&M University, the Lutheran brotherhood, the dairy industry, and everyone else who knew him in person, by reputation, by virtue of his beneficence, or through the enjoyment of Blue Bell Ice Cream.

Our good and humble friend rests in peace.

[Appendix One]
Edisms

1. No one ever gets lost on a straight road.

2. It's important to do what's right and ethical, not merely what's legal.

3. Integrity is not negotiable.

4. There's no telling how much good you can do if you don't mind who gets the credit.

5. You can whip almost any problem if you work hard enough and long enough.

6. Few people have original thoughts, so it's wise to take ideas from others and put them together.

7. Aptitude is important, but so is attitude.

8. Each of us was put on Earth for some good reason.

9. It's good to be benevolent.

10. Moderation is the key.

11. It's a cinch by the inch, hard by the yard.

12. It's more blessed to give than to receive.

13. Admit your mistakes—with its corollary: Forget excuses.

14. Keep things in perspective.

15. Maintain a sense of humor.

16. Don't assume. (It makes an "ass" out of "u" and "me.")

17. Learn to communicate effectively.

18. Work hard—the harder you work, the luckier you get.

19. Hire honor students for administrative positions.

20. Do not compromise your principles.

21. Thank people who have helped you.

22. Be honest in all your dealings.

23. Never do anything that your conscience tells you is wrong.

24. If you can do some good, do it now.

25. Be prepared.

26. Do what you say you're going to do.

27. Stand up for what's right.

28. Be strong enough to delay gratification.

29. Follow the Golden Rule. (Do unto others as you would have them do unto you.)

30. Work, don't worry.

31. Do a common job uncommonly well.

32. Think ahead.

33. Set goals and work toward them.

34. It's good to be humble.

[Appendix Two]
In Ed's Own Words

The following statements are a few excerpts from a variety of Ed. F. Kruse's speeches, interviews, notes, and other comments. They cover several topics.

THOUGHTS ON WHY BLUE BELL IS IN BUSINESS:

1. To make products that offer a combination of price, quality, variety, and service through friendly and trustworthy people who will make our company the best in our industry from which to buy.

2. To establish wages, working conditions, benefits, job security, opportunity, and personal recognition that combined will make our company the best in our industry with which to work.

3. To offer our stockholders a greater return on their investment and greater security than they can obtain elsewhere in our industry.

4. To demonstrate that Blue Bell is a good neighbor and citizen by our active support of good government, education, health programs, and other good works that benefit the entire community in which we operate.

THOUGHTS ON BLUE BELL'S STRENGTHS:

Blue Bell has excellent products, thanks to Howard Kruse, but people are the most important asset that the company has. Blue Bell is fortunate to have excellent people and they are the right people: Round pegs for round holes and square pegs for square holes.

· · · · ·

Blue Bell's greatest possession is its brand name—Blue Bell Ice Cream from the little creamery in Brenham.

• • • • •

Blue Bell stresses character, honesty, integrity, love, concern, absence of jealousy, and helping others.

• • • • •

Continuity of management has also been a big advantage for us, as there have been only four CEOs or managers in the past 94 years.

• • • • •

Blue Bell has been innovative, setting the trend instead of following. We were the first in Texas to make frozen yogurt and the first anywhere to make sugar-free ice cream, Homemade Vanilla, Cookies 'n Cream, Rainbow Freeze Bars, Mini Snacks, and many other products.

• • • • •

Do you know how we get new flavor ideas? We have fifty branches, and each one comes up with new flavors to suggest. Some individuals may actually make the flavor—stir it up. The ideas float up to the regional managers. The research and development department comes up with other flavors. Then, there is a vote. This past year there were 160 flavor combinations for them to consider. That blows my mind. I think if you ask twenty-five people what their favorite flavor is, you'll get twenty-two different answers.

• • • • •

Our product is a consumer-driven product. We advertise and give service. We make every product the best way we know and then price it to stores from our costs. It may be higher or lower than competition, but it offers real value.

• • • • •

Each consumer who purchases a half-gallon is a separate consumer. The fact we produced and sold 999 well-packaged products does not impress the one in 1,000 purchasers who might get one below Blue Bell quality standards.

THOUGHTS ON MANAGING BLUE BELL:

If employees want to talk, they can come in and talk. Our door is wide open. It always has been. If they've got a problem, hey, let's sit down and talk about it. There's an answer to it. We've tried to operate that way all the way through.

．　．　．　．　．

Making a profit is necessary to stay in business, but doing so at all costs is absolutely wrong. Companies must have leaders they can trust. Companies need to have leaders with a vision, who communicate to employees and stockholders what their goals are and how they plan to get there. Our employees, customers, suppliers, and consumers need to be treated as we would like to be treated. We will never ask employees to do anything morally or legally wrong. We are in business for the long haul, not for what makes us look good only today.

．　．　．　．　．

I enjoy making decisions. When I played football in high school I was quarterback. There was nothing that I liked better than to call signals. And I don't like to be so autocratic that I can say, "I am the only person that knows what the answer is." As a matter of fact, far from it because I know I don't know the answers to everything. But I do like to call on subordinates. I like their opinions, and if it gets to a heavy decision, I like as many opinions as I can get. We try to weigh what those opinions are. We vote on a lot of things. . . . And if I get outvoted, I don't feel bad, and I don't think any of my employees do or really should either. And I am inclined to go their way. There is only one thing that I feel like I can do if I want to, and I have invoked it one time where I have said, "It is the president's prerogative, fellows; we are going to do this." And the only time where I really invoked that prerogative and I was badly outnumbered, they proved I was wrong.

．　．　．　．　．

I have worn all the hats, but as time has passed, I've learned to delegate responsibilities and rely on the excellent people I've put in place. Nevertheless, having performed the duties myself, I know what my staff is facing and can advise well.

．　．　．　．　．

The buck stops here—just like President Truman said.

．　．　．　．　．

As Blue Bell continues to grow, it becomes more and more important for us to help educate our new employees on just who and what Blue Bell is. Many of the values and practices we maintain can be traced back to my father, E. F.

Kruse, who managed the company from 1919 until his early death in 1951. And my outlook on running a business, as well as my brother's, can be traced directly back to the lessons he taught us. He was a very straight and fairminded man. I never heard him curse—not even once. He followed Christian principles and the Golden Rule. Because his background was in education, he was very good at teaching those around him important lessons, and making them stick. . . . The lessons of hard work, honesty, and wise spending were ones that have benefited Howard and me well and have helped set the course for continued success in our company.

•   •   •   •   •

Lessons for the sales team:

1. Have a specific purpose for calling on a customer.

2. Know the customer's business and be prepared to tweak your call so that your suggestions apply directly to him.

3. Be sure you arrive on time for your appointment.

4. Treat the customer with utmost respect.

5. Maintain eye contact.

6. Ask for new business—increased freezer space, more flavors, new product lines, end-caps, special sales, ads, point-of-purchase signage, etc.

7. Demonstrate how these additions will increase the customer's profits, turnover, foot traffic, and sales. For example, I wonder how much more traffic you get when Blue Bell is on sale? Or, I wonder how much customers pick up in other products when they shop Blue Bell's sales? Or, I wonder how much of a better profit you would make if you gave Blue Bell only two feet more of space?

8. Provide facts on Blue Bell's turnover rate.

9. Refer to Blue Bell's success via Nielsen Reports.

10. Mention another similar establishment by name. Make sure it is not in direct competition with the customer at hand. Explain how the other establishment decided to increase its presence with Blue Bell and what benefits they have reaped.

11. Be positive. Realize that buyers find reasons not to buy. Be ready to counter those arguments.

12. Realize that an objection is a request for more information.

13. Communicate throughout the entire process so the customer will be kept up to date and informed.

14. Work, don't worry; i.e., avoid being shy or lazy. If you don't take the risk, you will never get the new business.

15. Avoid complacency or taking a customer for granted. Continue to treat each customer with utmost care, service, and respect.

16. Remember names and facts about the customer and other people who work in the establishment.

17. Remember that you are the public image for Blue Bell wherever you go.

18. Be ready to go back with new ideas and products.

19. Twenty percent of salespeople make 80 percent of sales. Count yourself in that 20 percent.

20. It's a cinch by the inch, hard by the yard.

•   •   •   •   •

I feel fortunate because I hope I have had something to do with giving 2,700 people an opportunity for employment and a chance to advance or grow, so they might enjoy life and provide for their families. These people have become good citizens, and many give of themselves and their talents to help others.

THOUGHTS ON HIRING:

Grades do not indicate intelligence, but they do indicate work ethic.

•   •   •   •   •

#1 Blue Bell wants to hire honest, sincere, enthusiastic, and capable employees. Attitude is very important.

#2 Qualifications for the particular job are important, but if the person has great #1 qualities, he can often be taught the skills he or she needs.

•   •   •   •   •

In my opinion, I believe
1. Hard work and study can be more fun than anything.
2. Extraordinary effort is always worthwhile.
3. The will and ability to do comes with the knowledge that you can do.

THOUGHTS ON CHALLENGES TO BLUE BELL:

A farmer once said, "The hardest thing about milking cows is that they never stay milked." There are days at Blue Bell that seem exactly like that. The ice cream never gets finally "made" once and for all; you have to keep making it every day. The Vitalines never catch up, equipment maintenance never ends, stores need to be restocked, and customers keep on messing up the displays.

Sometimes we wish for a more comfortable, trouble-free job. Or we think if we just get promoted one more rung, we would be free of some of the daily worries of dealing with machinery or maintaining the quality of raw ingredients or keeping all the store managers happy on our particular route.

It doesn't work that way. The higher-paying job brings tougher problems to handle. And, if we stop to consider, would we really want it any other way? It's the challenge of any job that gives it spice. Solving problems is the only way to find out how capable we really are and show what we can do. If you regard a difficult coworker or an impossible deadline as a challenge to be resolved with all your skill and ingenuity, that makes it kind of fun and keeps the job interesting.

• • • • •

There is no need trying to cover everything at one time. Take what you are doing and do it well, and then proceed to the next.

THOUGHTS ON HONESTY:

Highest compliment on a Blue Bell employee: "They do what they say they will do!"

• • • • •

For a company to be respected, it must practice honesty. Our company's personality is reflected by the sum of all employees. Each encounter one of our employees has with a consumer, a customer, or a sales rep builds upon our reputation. Company service is a reflection of honesty. When we tell customers we will service their store four times per week, we need to do this without fail or advise them in advance that, because of a problem, we cannot meet that requirement this week. Products also reflect honesty. When we tell consumers our Blue Bell Buttered Pecan Ice Cream has pecans in every bite, they know they can expect exactly what we say. Blue Bell has built an honest reputation over the years. Let's keep up the honest work.

THOUGHTS ON RELATIONSHIPS WITH OTHERS:

Every day we have an opportunity to make a difference in someone else's life. Every look, every word, and every action we have with those around us impacts them in one way or another. We are charged with the enormous responsibility of deciding what impact we choose to make on each other.

THOUGHTS ON COMPETITION:

If you have a problem, you can solve it if you work hard enough and long enough. It may not be the perfect answer, but you can come up with an answer. It just takes a lot of work. It's a challenge. If you're competitive and you want to win, you can do it. You can beat it.

• • • • •

I've said many times through the years that Blue Bell is a special company because of the people who work here. We've made it our goal to find new and better ways of working together and putting the needs of others first. Now we're about to apply that principle in relation to one of our competitors. Wells Blue Bunny Ice Cream Company is one of the largest independent ice cream companies in the United States. Recently, one of its two plants in Le Mars, Iowa, sustained a major ammonia leak and subsequent blast that has completely shut down the plant. Even though they are one of our competitors, we feel the humanitarian thing to do is to help them out by producing some products for them.

• • • • •

A STORY THAT APPEALED TO BOTH E. F. KRUSE AND ED KRUSE

The following story was found in Ed's files, but it was originally in E. F.'s files because it is dated 1925. It was written by J. Kindleberger of the Kalamazoo Vegetable Parchment Company in Kalamazoo, Michigan, on June 23, 1925. It must have been an inspirational tale for both Kruses, because they both held on to it.

Cinders on the Track
Gentlemen:
As this is a true story, please visualize a country schoolhouse standing at the top of a long hill which ran back and down into a field owned by a crabbed old man who hated dogs and disliked boys. One winter, and this happened approximately 40 years ago, rain, snow, and following these, zero weather, had made of this hill an ideal coasting place. Every morning before school, every noon at recess, and at night when school was dismissed, a dozen or fifteen of us boys would have the time of our young lives coasting down and dragging our sleds up this long icy hill. It wouldn't have been very much fun for one boy to do this all alone by himself, because without company the hill would have been too steep for him to climb. One night as we gathered

at the top of the hill, we found that the old gentleman had covered the ice with cinders and ashes. There is some fruit that mellows and sweetens with age, but a persimmon is always a persimmon. We were mad, rip roaring mad. Every boy in the bunch, with one exception, suggested ways and means whereby we might "get even," but this lad said, "What we fellows want to do is to slide, and throwin' stones at his house ain't goin' to help us none; there's a bunch of shingles over there, let's all grab one and clean off the cinders." Somebody is always throwing cinders on your track. Somebody is always saying and doing mean things. Somebody is always unfair competition. It always has been so and it always will be so, but the man who slides along with the least friction and the greatest success, is the man who, smilingly grabbing the shingle of quality and fair dealing, shovels off the cinders. The success that comes by overcoming obstacles is the only one success that really counts.

Sincerely yours,

KALAMAZOO VEGETABLE PARCHMENT COMPANY
J. Kindleberger

Ed quotes a favorite message from Mother Teresa, "Spread love everywhere you go: first of all in your own house. Give love to your children, to your wife or husband, to the next-door neighbor. . . . Let no one ever come to you without leaving better and happier. Be the living expression of God's kindness; kindness in your face, kindness in your eyes, kindness in your smile, kindness in your warm greeting."

•   •   •   •   •

A STORY ED LIKES TO SHARE WITH OTHERS:

This story was written by Dan Clark:

A friend of mine named Paul received an automobile from his brother as a Christmas present. On Christmas Eve when Paul came out of his office, a street urchin was walking around the shiny new car, admiring it. "Is this your car, Mister?" he asked.

Paul nodded and said, "My brother gave it to me for Christmas."

The boy was astounded. "You mean your brother gave it to you and it didn't cost you nothing? Boy, I wish. . . ." He hesitated. Of course Paul knew what he was going to wish for. He was going to wish he had a brother like that. But what the lad said jarred Paul all the way down to his heels. "I wish," the boy went on, "that I could be a brother like that."

Paul looked at the boy in astonishment. Then impulsively he added, "Would you like to take a ride in my automobile?"

"Oh yes, I'd love that," he replied. After a short ride, the boy turned and with his eyes aglow, said, "Mister, would you mind driving in front of my house?" Paul smiled a little. He thought he knew what the lad wanted. He wanted to show his neighbors that he could ride home in a big automobile. But Paul was wrong again. "Will you stop where those two steps are?" the boy asked. He ran up the steps. Then in a little while Paul heard him coming back, but he was not coming fast. He was carrying his little crippled brother. He sat him down on the bottom step, then sort of squeezed up against him and pointed to the car. "There she is, Buddy, just like I told you upstairs. His brother gave it to him for Christmas and it didn't cost him a cent. And some day I'm gonna give you one just like it. . . . Then you can see for yourself all the pretty things in the Christmas windows that I've been trying to tell you about."

Paul got out and lifted the lad to the front seat of his car. The shining-eyed older brother climbed in beside him and the three of them began a memorable holiday ride. That Christmas Eve, Paul learned what Jesus meant when he said, "It is more blessed to give. . . ."

THOUGHTS ON LIVING IN THE PRESENT:

You know you feel good today and you feel like you're going to live forever. That's not necessarily true. You never know. And, every day you're here, you're just fortunate to have one more day. All I can say is that if there is any good for me to do, let me do it now for I may not pass this way again. That's the way it is.

THOUGHTS ON RETIREMENT:

Some people are old at 40; others are young at 80. As long as we can keep our power to wonder and to be able and eager to feel surprise and delight at each new discovery of mind or heart and keep our sense of humor and our desire to help others, we will be ever young at heart.

• • • • •

I never expect to retire 100 percent. . . . I don't want to be a problem to anybody at this company. . . . I would like for somebody here to save some kind of an office or cubbyhole for me to crawl into to open my mail. I would try not to be a bother to everybody—if I can be of assistance, if I can give information or counsel anybody, etc., then fine.

• • • • •

[Appendix Three]
An Ed. F. Kruse and Blue Bell Creameries Time Line

1848   Ed Kruse's maternal grandfather Henry Quebe is born in Germany on November 18.

1853   Ed's paternal grandfather August Kruse is born in Hunteburg, Germany, on October 26.

1854   Ed's maternal grandmother Bertha Schlottmann is born on September 19 in the Salem community near Brenham, Texas.

1864   Ed's paternal grandmother Wilhelmine Lippe is born in Dieligen, Germany, on March 26.

1865   Ed's maternal grandfather Henry Quebe emigrates from Germany and settles in the Salem community near Brenham, Texas.

1871   Ed's paternal grandparents August Kruse and Wilhelmine Lippe emigrate with their families from Germany and settle in the Prairie Hill community near Brenham, Texas.

1872   Ed's maternal grandparents Henry Quebe and Bertha Schlottmann elope in the Salem community near Brenham, Texas.

1882   Ed's paternal grandparents August Kruse and Wilhelmine Lippe marry on December 22, 1882, in Prairie Hill, Texas.

1895   Ed's father E. F. Kruse is born on April 20 in the Prairie Hill community near Brenham, Texas.

1897   Ed's mother Bertha Quebe is born on February 13 in the Cedar Hill community near Brenham, Texas.

1901   Evelyn Kruse's father Ewald Tiaden is born on November 8.

1902   Evelyn Kruse's mother Hildegard Steinbach is born on July 25 in Cedar Hill near Brenham, Texas.

1907   The Brenham Creamery Company is incorporated to make butter from extra cream produced by the cows of area farmers.

1911   The Brenham Creamery Company begins to produce ice cream—2 gallons per day maximum.

1919   E. F. Kruse is hired to manage the Brenham Creamery Company.

1920   E. F. Kruse marries Bertha Quebe on January 22.

1921   Ed's older sister Bertha Kruse is born on January 8.

1923   Ed's older sister Mildred Louise Kruse is born on March 6.

1924   Ed's paternal grandfather August Kruse dies on October 28.

1925   Ed's maternal grandfather Henry Quebe dies on February 17.

1927   Ed's older sister Edwina is born on April 2 but succumbs to whooping cough on May 3.

1928   Ed. F. (Edward Fred) Kruse is born on March 15 to E. F. and Bertha Quebe Kruse.

1928   Evelyn Tiaden Kruse's parents Ewald Tiaden and Hildegard Steinbach marry on April 28 and settle in the Stone community near Brenham.

1929   Evelyn Delores Tiaden is born on March 25 to Ewald and Hildegard Steinbach Tiaden.

1930   Ed's younger brother Howard W. Kruse is born on August 1.

1930   E. F. Kruse changes the name of the Brenham Creamery Company to Blue Bell Creameries.

1930   Blue Bell Creameries opens a second butter plant in Giddings, Texas.

1934   Ed's younger sister Evelyn Ann Kruse is born on May 13.

1936   Blue Bell purchases its first refrigerated truck and continuous freezer.

1938   Ed's paternal grandmother Wilhelmine "Mina" Kruse dies on February 4.

1939   Pint ice cream containers are used for the first time.

1941   Ed, 13, and Howard, 11, begin working part-time at Blue Bell.

1941   Ed's maternal grandmother Bertha Quebe dies on June 7.

1945   Ed graduates from Brenham High School.

1949   Ed receives his BS in dairy manufacturing from Texas A&M University.

1949   Ed begins working at Swift and Company as an ice cream salesman.

1950   Ed marries Evelyn Tiaden on June 18.

1951   Ed joins Blue Bell full-time as a route supervisor.

1951   Ed and Evelyn's daughter Karen Kruse is born on June 3.

1951   E. F. Kruse dies on October 21 at Methodist Hospital in Houston.

1951   Ed becomes manager and secretary/treasurer of Blue Bell.

1952   Blue Bell produces mellorine and Blue Bell Supreme Ice Cream.

1952   Blue Bell Supreme is produced in pint and half-gallon containers

1952   Howard Kruse receives his BS in dairy manufacturing from Texas A&M.

1952   Howard Kruse reports to duty in Korea.

1952   Ed joins Brenham Rotary Club and remained an active member until his death.

1953   Ed and Evelyn's son Ken Kruse is born on May 12.

1954   Howard Kruse joins Blue Bell Creameries full-time.

1954   Ed and Evelyn's son Paul Kruse is born on October 7.

1956   Howard Kruse becomes assistant general manager of Blue Bell.

1956   Ed closes Giddings butter plant.

1957   Blue Bell celebrates its 50th anniversary.

1958   Blue Bell quits making butter and concentrates on ice cream.

1958   Blue Bell's ice cream sales reach $1 million annually.

1958   Ed arranges for key employees to purchase stock in Blue Bell.

1958   Ed and Evelyn's son Neil Kruse is born on April 7.

1958   Ed serves as president of Brenham Rotary Club.

1960   Ed hires John Barnhill Jr. to guide sales in the new Houston market.

1960   Marvin Giese tends to vending machine business in Houston.

1960   Houston becomes Blue Bell Branch #1.

1962   John Barnhill opens first permanent branch facility in Houston.

1965   Clarence Jaster leads Blue Bell's entry into Austin—Branch #2.

1965   Howard Kruse installs first Vitaline for automated making of frozen snacks.

1966   Ed serves as president of Brenham Industrial Foundation.

1967   Blue Bell begins jobbing operations with Baby Ruth Ice Cream Bar.

1968   Ed becomes president and chairman of the board of Blue Bell.

1968 Howard Kruse adds secretary to his title of assistant general manager.

1969 Howard Kruse develops Blue Bell Homemade Vanilla Ice Cream.

1969 Lyle Metzdorf begins steering Blue Bell's advertising.

1969 Ed is named chairman of the board of First National Bank.

1971 Ed's sister Bertha Kruse Spitzer dies on January 28.

1971 Eugene Supak joins Howard in the production area of the company.

1971 Blue Bell sales reach the $5 million mark.

1971 Ed is elected to the board of the International Association of Ice Cream Manufacturers.

1972 Blue Bell builds modern new plant on Loop 577 in Brenham.

1972 Little Creamery concentrates on making frozen snacks.

1972 John Barnhill returns to Brenham as first general sales manager.

1973 Melvin Ziegenbein takes Blue Bell into Beaumont—Branch #3.

1973 Ed serves as president of Dairy Products Institute of Texas.

1974 Blue Bell sales reach the $10 million mark.

1977 Girl and cow logo is introduced.

1977 Gold, silver, and white rims reflect relative costs of ingredients.

1978 Evelyn Kruse's father Ewald Tiaden dies on June 19.

1978 Melvin Ziegenbein takes Blue Bell into Dallas—Branch #4.

1978 Howard develops Cookies 'n Cream Ice Cream for ice cream parlors.

1978 Ed begins three-year term as president of the Dixie Dairy Products Association.

1979 Ed begins 10-year service on Texas Lutheran University Board of Regents.

1980 Cookies 'n Cream becomes available for home market year-round.

1980 Branch #5 opens in Alvin, Texas.

1981 William J. Rankin Jr., CPA, joins Blue Bell; later becomes CFO.

1981 Branch #6 opens in Fort Worth, Texas.

1981 Blue Bell reaches $50 million in sales.

1982 Branch #7 opens in North Dallas, Texas.

1982 Branch #8 opens in Humble, Texas.

1982 Ed is elected vice chairman of the International Association of Ice Cream Manufacturers.

1983   Ed begins three-year term as chairman of International Association of Ice Cream Manufacturers.

1984   Ed survives airplane crash in Presidio, Texas, on February 15.

1984   Branch #9 opens in San Antonio, Texas.

1984   Blue Bell sales top $100 million.

1985   Branch #10 opens in South Dallas, Texas.

1985   Blue Bell sets up portable dipping stations in hospitals, malls, schools.

1986   Paul Kruse joins Blue Bell as legal counsel.

1986   Ed cuts back hours to four days per week, becomes CEO, and continues as chairman of the board of directors.

1986   Ed begins 15-year service on board of Lutheran Foundation of South.

1986   Howard Kruse becomes president of Blue Bell.

1986   John Barnhill becomes executive vice president.

1986   Branch #11 opens in East Texas (Longview).

1986   Branch #12 opens in Waco, Texas.

1987   Blue Bell brings advertising in-house, with Metzdorf advising.

1987   Ed is named Washington County Man of the Year.

1988   New corporate headquarters and visitors' center open in Brenham.

1988   Branch #13 opens in Corpus Christi, Texas.

1989   Diet Blue Bell appears—first half-gallon flavor made with NutraSweet in the United States.

1989   Branch #14 opens in Oklahoma City—first branch outside Texas.

1989   Branch #15 opens in Baton Rouge, Louisiana.

1989   Record 100,000 visitors tour Blue Bell's plant and visitors' center.

1989   Market share is 60 percent in Houston, Dallas/Fort Worth, and San Antonio.

1990   Blue Bell distributes products in Mexico through Paletas Manhattan.

1990   Branch #16 opens in Tulsa, Oklahoma.

1990   Branch #17 opens in West Texas (Big Spring).

1991   Half-gallon carton design is slightly altered—still features cow and girl.

1991   Branch #18 opens in New Orleans, Louisiana.

1991   Branch #19 opens in the Rio Grande Valley (Harlingen, Texas).

1991   E. F. and Bertha Kruse Village—a retirement community in Brenham—opens thanks to contributions from their children.

1992   Ed receives Distinguished Service Award from Texas Lutheran University.

1992   Branch #20 opens in Ruston, Louisiana.

1992   Third production facility opens—in Broken Arrow, Oklahoma.

1993   E. F., Ed, and Howard Kruse are inducted into the Texas Business Hall of Fame.

1993   Branch #21 opens in Kansas City, Kansas.

1993   Ed cuts back hours to two days per week; remains chairman of the board.

1993   Howard Kruse becomes CEO.

1994   Branch #22 opens in Mobile, Alabama.

1994   Ed begins six-year term as chairman of the board of trustees of the Lutheran Foundation of the South.

1995   Mini Frozen Snacks becomes nation's first line of bite-sized snacks in that category.

1995   Ed is named Lutheran of the Year by Lutheran Social Services of the South.

1995   Ed is inducted into the Dairy Products Institute Hall of Fame.

1995   Branch #23 opens in Jackson, Mississippi.

1995   Branch #24 opens in Montgomery, Alabama.

1995   Branch #25 opens in Birmingham, Alabama.

1996   Ed's mother Bertha Quebe Kruse dies on January 3.

1996   New three-story production facility is completed in Brenham.

1996   Blue Bell purchases Flav-O-Rich Ice Cream plant in Sylacauga, Alabama.

1996   Homemade Vanilla Light Ice Cream is introduced.

1997   Renovated Sylacauga, Alabama plant begins production.

1997   Branch #26 opens in Little Rock, Arkansas.

1997   Branch #27 opens in Huntsville, Alabama.

1997   Branch #28 opens in New Braunfels, Texas.

1998   Ed receives the Soaring Eagle Award from International Association of Ice Cream Manufacturers.

1998   Branch #29 opens in Atlanta (East), Georgia.

1998   Branch #30 opens in Atlanta (West), Georgia.

1998   Branch #31 opens in North Texas (Lewisville).

1998   Branch #32 opens in Memphis, Tennessee.

1998   Melvin Ziegenbein is named general sales manager.

1998   New Blue Bell website goes online (www.bluebell.com).

1999   Ed and Evelyn's son Dr. Ken Kruse dies April 1.

1999   Branch #33 opens in Lafayette, Louisiana.

2000   John Barnhill retires.

2000   Branch #34 opens in Atlanta (South), Georgia.

2001   Branch #35 opens in Jacksonville, Florida.

2001   Blue Bell Aquatic Center opens.

2001   Ed receives Doctor of Humane Letters (*honoris causa)* from Texas
        Lutheran University.

2002   Lyle Metzdorf dies on February 18.

2002   Ed receives the Outstanding Alumnus Award from the College of
        Agriculture and Life Science at Texas A&M.

2002   Ed receives Ruby McSwain Outstanding Philanthropist Award from
        the National Agricultural Alumni and Development Association.

2002   Herbert and Letha Hohlt Park is dedicated in Brenham.

2002   Branch #36 opens in Lufkin, Texas.

2002   Branch #37 opens in Tallahassee, Florida.

2003   Ed and Evelyn's son Dr. Neil Kruse dies on August 11.

2003   Ed is inducted into the Corps of Cadets Hall of Honor at Texas
        A&M.

2003   Melvin Ziegenbein becomes vice president of sales and marketing.

2003   Ricky Dickson becomes general sales manager.

2003   Ed receives Sam Houston Sanders Corps of Cadets Hall of Honor
        Award.

2003   Branch #38 opens in Orlando, Florida.

2003   Branch #39 opens in Tampa, Florida.

2004   Howard Kruse retires; becomes president emeritus.

2004   Paul Kruse becomes president and CEO of Blue Bell.

2004   Jim Kruse, controller and Howard's son, becomes secretary of Blue Bell.

2004   Ed is named Distinguished Alumnus of Brenham High School.

2004   Branch #40 opens in El Paso, Texas.

2004   Branch #41 opens in Charlotte, North Carolina.

2005   Ed is named Distinguished Alumnus at Texas A&M.

2005   Ed and Howard Kruse receive Entrepreneur of the Year Award from Ernst and Young.

2005   Branch #42 opens in (East) Phoenix, Arizona.

2005   Branch #43 opens in Nashville, Tennessee.

2005   Ed, Howard, and Paul Kruse receive Kupfer Distinguished Executive Award from Mays Business School at Texas A&M.

2006   Ed is inducted into the Brenham Cubs Hall of Honor.

2006   Branch #44 opens in Columbia, South Carolina.

2007   Blue Bell celebrates its 100th anniversary.

2007   Evelyn Kruse's mother Hildegard Steinbach Tiaden dies on April 1.

2007   The Ed and Howard Kruse Field House at Brenham High School opens.

2007   Ed and Howard Kruse receive Distinguished Texas Awards at Agriculture Forum.

2007   Branch #45 opens in Louisville, Kentucky.

2008   Branch #46 opens in Katy, Texas.

2008   Branch #47 opens in Southwest Florida.

2009   Blue Bell purchases former Brentex/Mount Vernon Mills facility.

2009   Branch #48 opens in Miami, Florida.

2009   Ed and Evelyn establish the Edward F. and Evelyn D. Kruse Scholarship for Education and Pre-Theology at Texas Lutheran University.

2010   Ed, Howard, and Blue Bell make significant donation to renovate Olsen Field at Texas A&M. The baseball stadium becomes known as Olsen Field at Blue Bell Park.

2010   Melvin Ziegenbein retires.

2010   Ricky Dickson becomes vice president of sales and marketing.

2010   Wayne Hugo becomes general sales manager.

2010   Ed establishes W. J. "Bill" Rankin Agricultural Complex at Blinn College in Brenham.

2011   Branch #49 opens in Denver, Colorado.

2011   Branch #50 opens in Indianapolis, Indiana.

2011   Branch #51 opens in Delray Beach, Florida.

2011   Branch #52 opens in North Fort Worth, Texas.

2011   Branch #53 opens in Shreveport, Louisiana.

2011   Ed receives the first Lifetime Achievement Award from the Texas A&M Lettermen's Association.

2011   Eugene Supak semi-retires.

2011   Greg Bridges becomes vice-president of plant operations.

2011   Blinn College Ex-Students' Association names Ed its Person of the Year.

2012   Record 200,000 visitors tour plant and visitors' center.

2012   Branch #54 opens in Albuquerque, New Mexico.

2012   Branch #55 opens in Raleigh, North Carolina.

2012   Newly renovated Olsen Field at Blue Bell Park opens on the Texas A&M campus.

2013   Eugene Supak retires.

2013   Branch #56 opens in Richmond, Virginia.

2013   Branch #57 opens in (West) Phoenix, Arizona.

2013   E. F. and Bertha Kruse's surviving children and their spouses make a generous gift to create Kruse Center—a new recreation, activities, and athletic facility—on the Brenham campus of Blinn College.

2013   Ed and Evelyn Kruse donate 100 acres in south Brenham for the establishment of the Brenham Family Park.

2014   Ed retires as chairman of the board at Blue Bell but remains a member of the board of directors.

2014   Paul Kruse becomes chairman of the board of Blue Bell Creameries.

2014   Ed Kruse Stadium—a softball facility—opens at Texas Lutheran University.

2014   Branch #58 opens in Knoxville, Tennessee.

2015   Evelyn and Ed Kruse, along with Verlin and Howard Kruse and Modesta and Clayton Williams Jr., receive the Sterling C. Evans Medal, the Texas A&M Foundation's highest honor.

[Appendix Four]
Facts You May Not Know About Ed. F. Kruse

His father—E. F. Kruse
His brother—Howard W. Kruse
His high school coach—Owen Erekson
His friend—President George H. W. Bush
Former Texas A&M football coach—R. C. Slocum

MENTORS

His father—E. F. Kruse
His mother—Bertha Quebe Kruse
His siblings—Bertha, Mildred, Howard, and Evelyn Ann
His Sunday school teachers
His coaches for competitive Ten Commandments sessions
His coaches for competitive softball
His high school teachers
His early office manager—Edna Ruppert

MOUNTAINTOP EXPERIENCES

His wedding day
The birth of each of his four children
Receiving the Distinguished Alumnus Award from Texas A&M
Spending time with President George H. W. Bush

Receiving the Lifetime Achievement Award from the Letterman's Association at Texas A&M

Height—5'11"
Weight—183 lbs.
Blood type—A Positive

Ate Blue Bell Ice Cream every day
Drove a little too fast
Ate lunch at home unless he had a meeting
Tried to eat nutritiously but was not a fanatic
Was not a vegetarian but included many vegetables in his meals
Maintained his weight by cutting back calories if scale went up three
    pounds
Fell asleep easily—within five minutes of his head hitting the pillow
Wore a coat and tie to work every day
Dressed in khaki trousers and a cotton shirt at home
Had several pairs of shoes that he liked to rotate on a daily basis
Made a decision by gathering facts, weighing them, and then choosing
    the best option
Tried to live all aspects of life in moderation

Blue Bell Ice Cream—Homemade Vanilla, but he liked them all
Meal—steak or fried chicken, gravy, potatoes, pork & beans, and a salad
Restaurant meal—barbequed baby-back ribs
Eating experience—seven days at Bill Sim's Lodge in Newhalen, Alaska,
    where he fished several times. The meals are served family-style—
    always with two entrees. It's impossible even to taste everything served.
Coffee—black
Candy bars—Hershey Almond Chocolate and Snickers
Cakes—Chocolate cake with chocolate icing; his mother's banana cake
    with its topping of sugar and banana slices
Mixed drink—Vodka tonic

Pro football team—Dallas Cowboys
College sports team—Texas A&M University Aggies
Car—usually a Chevrolet
Flowers—gloxinias or African violets
Television shows
   Wheel of Fortune
   The Price is Right
   Jeopardy!
   5:00 p.m. newscasts
   football games
   Masters Golf Tournament
   Tennis with Evelyn—U S Open, French Open, Wimbledon,
   Australian Open
Historical moment—Neil Armstrong walking on the moon—July 20,
   1969
Vacation spots
   St. Croix in the Virgin Islands
   Palm Springs, California
   Scottsdale, Arizona
Hotel room—Monteleone Hotel in New Orleans—all the rooms had
   sold out, so he got the honeymoon suite—gorgeous with white carpets
   throughout

DISLIKES

Being alone—preferred to be with other individuals or couples
Speeding tickets
Most perfumes and colognes
Omelets
Rainy days
Being told a lie

TEMPERAMENT

He was a doer.
He didn't procrastinate.
He didn't necessarily follow his instincts, but he paid close attention to
   them.
He was a bit impatient.

He was slightly hyperactive.

He wasn't jealous—he was happy for everyone to attain whatever he could; in fact, that might serve as an impetus to him, "Hey, maybe I can do just as well."

He was easy to get along with.

He didn't lie.

Bad grammar bothered him a bit.

BELIEFS

He believed in God and that Jesus Christ was his Savior.

Everyone should have a relationship with his God and do good for others.

There is a reason for each of us, and therefore we all need to contribute back to society.

He knew he was lucky, but he also felt that people tend to contribute to their own luck.

Love is the most moving force there is—no one ever died from receiving too much love.

POLITICS

President at birth—Calvin Coolidge

First president of Ed's memory—Franklin Delano Roosevelt

Presidents Ed met—Lyndon Baines Johnson, Ronald Reagan, George Herbert Walker Bush, George W. Bush

Political offices held—none, but considered running for mayor of Brenham once; the incumbent decided to run again and that suited Ed just fine

Party affiliation—voted for candidates who were in line with his viewpoints

Felt it is important for businesspeople to know the politicians on every level in order to inform them about proposed legislation and its effect on their industry, employees, and consumers

[Sources]

INTERVIEWS

Kruse, Bertha Quebe. Interview with Ed. F. Kruse. Brenham, Texas, June 26, 1983.

Kruse, Ed. F. Interview with Floyd Jenkins, North Texas University Business Archives Project. Brenham, Texas, August 18, 1983.

———. Interview with Dorothy M. MacInerney. Brenham, Texas, May 3, 2012.

———. Interview with Dorothy M. MacInerney. Brenham, Texas, May 23, 2012.

———. Interview with Dorothy M. MacInerney. Brenham, Texas, August 29, 2012.

———. Interview with Dorothy M. MacInerney. Brenham, Texas, September 28, 2012.

———. Interview with Dorothy M. MacInerney. Brenham, Texas, February 8, 2013.

———. Interview with Dorothy M. MacInerney. Brenham, Texas, February 27, 2013.

———. Interview with Dorothy M. MacInerney. Brenham, Texas, May 30, 2013.

———. Interview with Dorothy M. MacInerney. Brenham, Texas, November 20, 2013.

Kruse, Ed. F., and Howard W. Kruse. Interview with *Austin Business Journal*. Brenham, Texas, May 23, 2005.

Kruse, Ed. F., and Howard W. Kruse. "The Little Creamery: Two Men, One Legacy, and the Best Ice Cream in the Country." Interview with KBTX News. Brenham, Texas, May 24, 2010.

Kruse, Ed. F., and Ruth Goeke. Interview with Dorothy M. MacInerney. Brenham, Texas, February 24, 2014.

Goeke, Ruth. Interview with Dorothy M. MacInerney. Brenham, Texas, June 28, 2012.

Hall, Karen Kruse. Email exchange with Dorothy M. MacInerney. January 9, 2014.

———. Email exchange with Dorothy M. MacInerney. May 5, 2014.

———. Interview with Dorothy M. MacInerney. Austin, Texas, January 20, 2014.

———. Interview with Dorothy M. MacInerney. Austin, Texas, July 17, 2014.

———. Telephone interview with Dorothy M. MacInerney. March 7, 2014.

Hall, Karen Kruse, and Evelyn Tiaden Kruse. Interview with Dorothy M. MacInerney. College Station, Texas, February 2, 2014.

Senske, Kurt. Email exchange with Dorothy M. MacInerney. January 14, 2014.

ARTICLES

"100 Acres in South Brenham for Brenham Family Park." *Brenham Banner-Press*, December 18, 2013.

"2006–07 Annual Report: Story on Ed & Evelyn Kruse." *Texas Lutheran University President's Annual Report*, July 20, 2007.

"Aggie Tankmen Take DAC 41–34 for Fifth Straight: Green Unbeaten; Medley Trio Makes Pool Record." *The Battalion*, 1947.

Agness, Jack. "Years Mellow Sanders." *The Houston Post*, May 30, 1982.

"All About John [Barnhill]." *The Scoop,* September 1997.

Apple, R. W. Jr. "Making Texas Cows Proud." *The New York Times*, May 31, 2006.

Applewhite, Linda. "Texas Dairy Introduces First 3-D Frozen Novelties." *Shelby Report of the Southwest,* November 1980.

———. "The Little Creamery in Brenham." *Shelby Report of the Southwest,* November 1980.

Binz, Larry. "That Little Creamery in Brenham." *Texas Neighbors,* July 1989.

Blake, Tommy. "Avenge Last Year's Score at Navasota." *Brenham Banner-Press*, October 9, 1944.

———. "Brenham Cubs Are Second in District Meet: Great Bastrop Bears Clearly Outclass Other Schools." *Brenham Banner-Press*, March 19, 1945.

———. "Brenham Cubs Even Up Score with Waller." *Brenham Banner-Press*, January 10, 1945.

———. "Brenham Cubs Meet Yeguas Here Friday." *Brenham Banner-Press*, January 25, 1945.

———. "Brenham Cubs Take Caldwell by 19–8 Score—Visitors Get Huffy and Leave Before Game is Over." *Brenham Banner-Press*, February 12, 1945.

———. "Brenham High Will Meet La Grange in District Game Here." *Brenham Banner-Press*, October 12, 1944.

———. "Brenham Is Chosen as Place to Play Bi-District Game." *Brenham Banner-Press*, November 23, 1944.

———. "Brenham Wins Invitation Cage Tourney Here Saturday." *Brenham Banner-Press*, January 22, 1945.

———. "Bryan Victor Over Brenham in Extra Time." *Brenham Banner-Press*, January 31, 1945.

———. "Cubs Annex Two Contests from Blinn." *Brenham Banner-Press*, December 18, 1944.

———. "Cubs B Team Vanquished by Allen's Giants." *Brenham Banner-Press*, November 10, 1944.

———. "Cubs Beat Giddings 19–0 to Take Lead for District Title." *Brenham Banner-Press*, October 30, 1944.

———. "Cubs Defeat Consolidated by 24–0 Score—Cubs Look Good on Defense First Time of Year." *Brenham Banner-Press*, November 6, 1944.

———. "Cubs Defeat Navasota in Game There." *Brenham Banner-Press*, February 7, 1945.

———. "Cubs Defeat Sommerville by 72 to 12 Score." *Brenham Banner-Press*, January 29, 1945.

———. "Cubs Look Great as They Trample Bellville by Score of 38 to 6." *Brenham Banner-Press*, October 23, 1944.

———. "Cubs Lose Out to Champions in Area Tilt—Brenham Boys Lead Most of Game at Lockhart." *Brenham Banner-Press*, March 3, 1945.

———. "Cubs Losers to Bellville by 19–8—Illness of Kruse Proves Blow to Brenham." *Brenham Banner-Press*, January 15, 1945.

———. "Cubs of Brenham to Play Bellville There on Friday." *Brenham Banner-Press*, October 19, 1944.

———. "Cubs Open Grid Season Friday Night at Bryan." *Brenham Banner-Press*, September 21, 1944.

———. "Cubs Prepared for Bi-District Game Tomorrow." *Brenham Banner-Press*, December 7, 1944.

———. "Cubs Scared by La Grange in Hot Tilt." *Brenham Banner-Press*, October 16, 1944.

———. "Cubs Second in Track Meet at Kyle Field." *Brenham Banner-Press*, April 5, 1945.

———. "Cubs Tackle A&M High Here Friday." *Brenham Banner-Press*, November 2, 1944.

———. "Cubs Tangle with Pirates Friday Night." *Brenham Banner-Press*, December 14, 1944.

———. "Cubs to Meet Carmine Five Here Tonight—Practice Game Slated to Prepare for Regional Tilt." *Brenham Banner-Press*, February 27, 1945.

———. "Cubs to Play Bellville in District Title." *Brenham Banner-Press*, February 2, 1945.

———. "Cubs to Play Bryan Cougars Here Tonight." *Brenham Banner-Press*, January 30, 1945.

———. "Cubs to Play District Game at Navasota." *Brenham Banner-Press*, October 5, 1944.

———. "Cubs to Play El Campo Here on December 8th." *Brenham Banner-Press*, November 27, 1944.

———. "Cubs to Play Friday Night at Giddings—Strong Teams Meet in Important Contest." *Brenham Banner-Press*, October 16, 1944.

———. "Cubs Trounce Bellville by 51 to 14 Score—Avenge Early Season Defeat." *Brenham Banner-Press*, February 5, 1945.

———. "Cubs Trounce Caldwell in District Title." *Brenham Banner-Press*, January 24, 1945.

———. "Cubs Trounce Carmine Five by 58 to 31." *Brenham Banner-Press*, February 28, 1945.

———. "Cubs Waddle Through Mud to Easy Win." *Brenham Banner-Press*, November 27, 1944.

———. "Cubs Will Open Season at Home Tomorrow Night." *Brenham Banner-Press*, September 28, 1944.

———. "Cubs Win District Basketball Title in La Grange Meet." *Brenham Banner-Press*, February 26, 1945.

———. "Cubs Win District Championship with Smithville Game." *Brenham Banner-Press*, November 20, 1944.

———. "Cubs Winners in East Half of District." *Brenham Banner-Press*, February 19, 1945.

———. "El Campo Wins from Cubs by Score of 22 to 6—Ricebirds Capture Bi-District Title in Game Here." *Brenham Banner-Press*, December 12, 1944.

———. "Erekson's Boys Play Waller Tomorrow Night Here." *Brenham Banner-Press*, January 8, 1945.

———. "Kruse Superb as Cubs Crush Somerville High—Cub Forward Sets New Individual Mark for Scoring." *Brenham Banner-Press*, February 14, 1945.

———. "Morris Frank Says Brenham Cubs to be T Party Hosts." *Brenham Banner-Press*, October 9, 1944.

———. "Morris Frank Will Address Football Team." *Brenham Banner-Press*, April 30, 1945.

———. "Smith Proves Cubs' Undoing." *Brenham Banner-Press*, September 25, 1944.

———. "Sommer Stars on Offensive for Brenham." *Brenham Banner-Press*, October 2, 1944.

"Blue Bell and Greenbacks: $20 Million in Ice Cream." *Houston Chronicle*, August 14, 1977.

Blue Bell Creameries. "Company Time Line." 2013.

Blue Bell Creameries. "Plans for Construction of a New Office and Manufacturing Plant in Brenham." Press release, 1971.

"Blue Bell Creameries Ice Cream Is Popular in This Territory." *The Hempstead News* (Golden Anniversary Edition), 1939.

"Blue Bell Creameries, Inc., of Brenham." *Lower Colorado River Authority Annual Report*, 1988.

"Blue Bell Creameries to Build New Plant." *Houston Chronicle*, May 2, 1971.

"Blue Bell Plant to Open April '72." *Retail Grocer*, October 1971.

"Blue Bell: Quality Not Melting During Growth." *Dallas/Fort Worth Business*, August 14, 1978.

"Blue Bell to Expand into Dallas-Fort Worth Market." *Brenham Banner-Press*, February 8, 1978.

Brooks, Arthur C. "Giving Makes You Rich." *Conde Nast Portfolio*, November 11, 2007.

Byrne-Dodge, Teresa. "The Best Ice Cream in Texas." *Ultra*, August 1985.

"Children of E. F. Kruse and Their Spouses Gift Kruse Center." *Blinn College Communications*, June 2013.

"Class Favorites." "The Cub Growl" of the *Brenham Banner-Press*, March 12, 1945.

Coggins, Cheryl. "Cream of Summer Job Crop Requires Thermal Underwear." *Austin American-Statesman*, August 8, 1980.

"College of Agriculture Endowed Scholarships: Ed. F. Kruse." *The Texas Aggie*, November 1987.

"College Station Swimmers Set New Records at Houston Meet." *The Battalion*, July 15, 1947.

"Consolidate Two Texas Creameries." *Brenham Banner-Press*, 1930.

Crider, Kitty. "Blue Bell Cranks Out Hits: That's How Cookies Crumble for Brenham Creamery." *Austin American-Statesman*, April 13, 1982.

"Dippel, Thomas H. Sr." Editorial. *Brenham Banner-Press*, January 20, 1972.

Downing, Martha. "Texas Dairy Introduces First 3-D Frozen Novelties." *Dairy Field*, April 1980.

"Dr. IQ." www.archives.org/details/Dr. IQ

Eckermann, Jennifer. "Starting Salary was 7½ Cents an Hour [Elton 'Andy' Anderson.]" *The Scoop,* January 1984.

"Ed and Evelyn Kruse Make Big Park Land Donation." *Brenham Banner-Press,* December 18, 2013.

"Ed, Evelyn Kruse Establish Food Science Fellowship." *The Scoop,* April 2003.

"Ed Kruse Named Chairman of First National Bank Board." *Brenham Banner-Press,* January 17, 1969.

"Ed Kruse Recognized for 50 Years of Employment with Company During Annual Christmas Banquet." *The Scoop,* December 2001.

"Evelyn Tiaden and Rosalie Streng Honored." *Brenham Banner-Press,* June 15, 1950.

"Evelyn Tiaden Wed in Twilight Ceremony." *Brenham Banner-Press,* June 26, 1950.

Ferrell, David. "Tasteful Celebration." *The Texas Aggie,* May–June 2007.

Freeman, Diane. "Blue Bell to Market New Diet Dessert." *Houston Post,* January 8, 1989.

Garland, Susan. "Creameries Aim to Lick Competition: Blue Bell Dips into a Parlor Fight." *Advertising Age,* July 15, 1985.

Garrison, Bob. "Blue Bell Creameries, Inc.: Country Charisma." *Dairy & Frozen Foods,* April 1991.

"Gentle Handling Increases Sales for Ice Cream." *Refrigerated Transporter,* February 1969.

Gibson, Elise. "Brenham's Pride Is Waco's Joy." *Waco Tribune-Herald,* June 16, 1983.

Griffith, Dottie. "Blue Bell's Got a Secret." *Dallas Morning News,* August 24, 1978.

Hanlon, Patricia. "Location Cited as Reason for New Ice Cream Plant in Broken Arrow." *Broken Arrow-Coweta News,* January 11, 1990.

Hibbert, Mary Jo, and Sandra Barron. "Brazos Valley Ice Cream." *The Bryan-College Station Eagle,* June 5, 1977.

Hooper, Carl. "They'll Take Vanilla." *Houston Post,* September 17, 1972.

Inampudi, Naveen, and Debbie Z. Harwell. "Blue Bell: The Cream Rises to the Top." *Houston History,* Spring 2012.

"Innovative Plants, Frozen Desserts Category: Blue Bell Creameries, Brenham, Texas." *Dairy Field,* February 2003.

Jackson, Robyn. "Cream of the Crop: Dietitians Rank Diet Ice Creams." *Hattiesburg American,* March 13, 1991.

"James Liepke: 'If There Was a Job, I Was Ready to Go.'" *The Scoop,* November 1988.

"Japanese Stir Things Up in the Lone Star State." *The Scoop,* October 1991.

Jordan, Harvie. "Made in Texas with Hometown Pride." *Texas Department of Agriculture Quarterly,* Spring 1981.

Kegg, Mary. "Blue Bell Ringing Clear as Leader in Ice Cream." *The Clear Creek Citizen,* June 28, 1989.

Kennedy, Maggie. "Texans Surrender Their Tastebuds to Blue Bell." *Dallas Times Herald,* April 14, 1982.

Kennedy, Sarah. "Sales of Ice Cream Are Frozen in Place." *Dairy Foods,* January 2013.

King, James R. "Blue Bell Creameries Likes Small-Town Image." *Youngstown Vindicator,* October 7, 1983.

Kruse, Ed. F. "Chairman's Column." *The Scoop*, March 29, 1996.

———. "Chairman's Column: A Christmas Story." *The Scoop*, December 1995.

———. "Chairman's Column: Best Wishes to John [Barnhill]." *The Scoop*, March 2000.

———. "Chairman's Column: Blue Bell Success Contributed to 'Dare to be Different' Attitude." *The Scoop*, April 1996.

———. "Chairman's Column: Congratulations Dallas on 25 Years." *The Scoop*, November 2003

———. "Chairman's Column: Extending a Helping Hand." *The Scoop*, May 1999.

———. "Chairman's Column: Holidays Bring Chance to Make Difference." *The Scoop*, December 1997.

———. "Chairman's Column: Honesty Remains a Virtue." *The Scoop*, November 1998.

———. "Chairman's Column: Japan Issue took Two Years to Create, 26 Hours to Resolve, and Weeks to Die Down." *The Scoop*, October 1991.

———. "Chairman's Column: Nomination to Hall of Fame Is to Be Shared by All Employees." *The Scoop*, April 1993.

———. "Chairman's Column: New ESOP Plan Gives Employees a Stake in the Company's Success." *The Scoop*, January 1990.

———. "Chairman's Column: Standing Independent and Strong." *The Scoop*, August 2000.

———. "Chairman's Column: Staying on a Straight Road." *The Scoop*, November 2002.

———. "Chairman's Column: Taking Stock of Blue Bell Today." *The Scoop*, September 1997.

———. "Chairman's Column: The Best Decision I Ever Made." *The Scoop*, July 1997.

———. "Chairman's Column: The Blue Bell Way." *The Scoop*, April 1998.

———. "Chairman's Column: The Legacy of E. F. Kruse." The Scoop, March 1997.

———. "Chairman's Column: The Loss of a Great Friend [Lyle Metzdorf]." *The Scoop*, April 2002.

———. "Chairman's Column: The Power of People." *The Scoop*, February 1999.

———. "End-of-Year Presentation—on Miss Edna's semi-retirement." December 1959.

———. "President's Column." *The Scoop*, August 1975.

———. "President's Column." *The Scoop*, September 1976.

———. "President's Column." *The Scoop*, January 1979.

———. "President's Column." *The Scoop*, November 1979.

———. "President's Column: Staying Number One Takes Hard Work." *The Scoop*, August 1982.

———. "World's Greatest Secretary." *Brenham Banner-Press*, April 23, 1990.

"Kruse Endows Food Science Fellowship." Texas A&M AgriLife, March 26, 2003. www.agrilife.org

"Kruse Family Continues Commitment to Higher Education with Gift to Blinn College." Blinn College, June 18, 2013. www.blinn.edu/news

"Kruse Is Honored at Surprise Party on 17th Birthday." "The Cub Growl" of the *Brenham Banner-Press*, March 26, 1945.

"Kruses Dish Up Support for TLU." Texas Lutheran University, n.d.

"Kruse-Tiaden Attendants Named." *Brenham Banner-Press*, June 16, 1950.

"Kruse, Trevino Tee Off in Open." *The Scoop,* May 1989.

Leavenworth, Geoffrey. "Blue Bell: A Red-Hot Ice Cream Company." *Texas Business,* February 1979.

Lee, Steven H. "Little Creamery Image Belies Blue Bell's Growth." *Dallas Morning News*, October 11, 1987.

Lieb, Mary Ellen. "Blue Bell Creameries." *Dairy Foods,* September 1988.

———. "The Blue Bell Mystique." *Dairy Foods,* June 1988.

"Liepke to Lead Charge into Baton Rouge." *The Scoop,* March 1989.

Mack, Toni. "The Up & Comers: Blue Bell Creameries." *Forbes,* January 22, 1990.

Marks, Miles. "Blue Bell, Kruses Pledge $7 Million to Upgrade Texas A&M's Baseball Stadium." Marketing and Communications Archive, Texas A&M University, November 23, 2010.

"Melvin Ziegenbein Retires After 40 Plus Years." *The Scoop,* April 2010.

"Midland and Houston Donors Receive Texas A&M Foundation's Highest Honor: Jack E. Brown '46 and James K. B. Nelson '49." Texas A&M University press release, April 29, 2011. www.giving.tamu.edu

"Miss Evelyn Tiaden and Edward Kruse Honored." *Brenham Banner-Press*, June 13, 1950.

"Miss Evelyn Tiaden and Edward Kruse Honored by Sister of Groom at Home of Mrs. Garrett." *Brenham Banner-Press*, June 14, 1950.

"Movers & Shakers: Blue Bell Creameries, Brenham, Texas." *Dairy Foods*, April 1989.

Nations, Hugh. "Blue Bell Dips into New Marketing Area." *Bryan-College Station Eagle*, July 18, 1985.

"New Dean Takes Over in Business: Owen Homer Erekson." Texas Christian University press release, 2008.

"Official FAA Accident Report on PIPER PA 31-P Accident in Presidio, Texas, USA on 2/15/1984." www.aircrashed.com/accident/FTW84LA133

Peoples, Carol. "Finke Reflects on 20 Years at Blue Bell." *The Scoop*, July 1986.

Prelli, Tracey. "Blue Bell Mystique Turns Creamery into Legend." *The Scoop*, July 1986.

———. "Kramer Gives His View of Good Days Gone By." *The Scoop*, February 1986.

Rose, Joan. "City Lands $10 Million Ice Cream Creamery." *Broken Arrow Scout*, January 4, 1989.

Rosenblatt, George. "Blue Bell and Greenbacks: $20 Million in Ice Cream." *Houston Chronicle*, August 14, 1977.

Saal, Herbert. "Aggressive Marketing of Quality Product Requires Blue Bell Creamery to Construct 8,000,000-Gallons-a-Year Facility." *American Dairy Review*, July 1973.

Seay, Gregory. "Ice Cream Sales Leave Sweet Taste in Mouths of Blue Bell Officials." *Houston Post*, circa July 1985.

Skow, John. "They All Scream For It." *Time*, August 10, 1981.

Smith, Pamela Accetta. "True Blue: Blue Bell Creameries' Passion for Authenticity Creates a Truly Unique Consumer-driven Company." *Dairy Field*, January 2002.

Smith, Tumbleweed. "Blue Bell Ice Cream is Becoming Texas Favorite." 1989. www.tumbleweedsmith.com

Sonnier, Sue. "The Little Creamery in Brenham." *The Conroe Courier*, October 28, 1981.

Sowers, Leslie. "A Chilling Thought: Diet Blue Bell." *Houston Chronicle*, January 6, 1989.

"The Gold Rim: These Are the People that Keep Us Going [Elton 'Andy' Anderson, Vastine Pietsch, Raymond Warmke]." *The Scoop*, May 1986.

"The Rest of the Story: Kruse Matriarch Adds Her Input to the Story of Blue Bell." *The Scoop*, December 1990.

"The Story Behind the Legend, Part I: Little Creamery Opens with Humble Beginnings." *The Scoop,* March 1997.

"The Story Behind the Legend, Part II: Little Creamery Struggled, But Held on during Early Years." *The Scoop,* May 1997.

"The Story Behind the Legend, Part III." *The Scoop,* November 1997.

"Texas Dairy Products Group." *Brenham Banner-Press,* 1973.

Tichich, Betty. "New Dipping Station." *Houston Chronicle,* July 23, 1985.

"Wayne Hugo: '. . . It Was Blue Bell or Nothing Else.'" *The Scoop,* July 1988.

Whitehead, Tom. "Pierre Roberts Got Hit in Head by a Caldwell Hornet." "The Cub Growl" of the *Brenham Banner-Press,* February 12, 1945.

Williamson, Judy. "Ice Cream Scoop!" *Dallas Morning News,* August 14, 1983.

Wilson, Amy. "Cream Crop: Brenham Creamery, with Annual Sales Exceeding $100 Million, Isn't About to Cry Over Spilled Milk." *Texas Weekly Magazine,* February 9, 1986.

BOOKS

Dent, Jim. *Twelve Mighty Orphans: The Inspiring True Story of the Mighty Mites Who Ruled Texas Football.* New York: Thomas Dunne Books, 2007.

Dippel, Tieman H. Jr. *Instilling Values in Transcending Generations: Bringing Harmony to Cultures Through the Power of Conscience.* Brenham, Tex.: Texas Peacemaker Publications, 2008.

MacInerney, Dorothy M. *Blue Bell Ice Cream: A Century at the Little Creamery in Brenham, Texas, 1907–2007.* Austin: Texas Monthly Press, 2006.

Thomasma, Kenneth. *Naya Nuki: Shoshoni Girl Who Ran.* Jackson, Wyo.: Grandview Publishing Co., 1983.

SPEECHES

Kruse, Ed. F. Acceptance Speech for Award as Lutheran of the Year. 1995.

———. Acceptance Speech for Lifetime Achievement Award from the Texas A&M Lettermen's Association. Texas A&M University, College Station, Texas, September 7, 2011.

———. Acceptance Speech, 1993 Texas Business Hall of Fame Meeting. Houston, Texas, October 7, 1993.

———. "Attitude-Aptitude." Speech to unknown audience, n.d.

———. "Be Prepared." Speech to unknown audience, n.d.

———. "Blinn Talk." Speech to audience at Blinn College, March 24, 1998.

———. "Can We Make Waves Without Rocking the Boat?" Speech to the Southwestern Dairy Industry Conference, Dallas, Texas, 1976.

———. "CEO Council Talk." Speech to a group of CEOs, January 31, 2000.

———. "Company Facts" and personal written notes for speech to unknown audience, 1993.

———. National Honor Society Talk at Brenham High School. Speech at the induction of new members to the Brenham High School National Honor Society, Brenham, Texas, November 3, 2004.

———. "Remarks of the President." Speech to the Southwestern Dairy Industry Conference, Dallas Texas, 1970.

———. Speech to a Group of Texas A&M Alumni. Texas A&M University, College Station, Texas, September 14, 2006.

———. Texas A&M Marketing Speech. Rudy Nayga's agribusiness marketing classes, Texas A&M University, College Station, Texas, October 6, 1998.

———. "The Dairy Industry—Present and Future." Speech to the Dairy Products Institute of Texas Conference at Texas Tech University, Lubbock, Texas, November 10, 1969.

LETTERS

Crow, John David. John David Crow to Ed. F. Kruse, February 24, 1997.

Illes, George M. George M. Iles of A. E. Iles Company to Ed. F. Kruse, February 28, 1952.

Kindleberger, J. J. Kindleberger of the Kalamzoo Vegetable Parchment Co. to E. F. Kruse and including the story "Cinders on the Track," June 25, 1925.

Kruse, Ed. F. Ed. F. Kruse to Brian Wright upon his becoming an Eagle Scout, n.d.

———. Ed. F. Kruse to Gene Summers, friend from Texas A&M University, April 28, 1985.

———. Ed. F. Kruse to staff at *Texas Aggie* magazine answering questions for article on 2005 Distinguished Alumnus Award, July 2005.

Strawser, Jerry. Jerry Strawser, Dean of the Mays Business School at Texas A&M University, to Paul Kruse, August 23, 2005.

OBITUARIES

Bridges, Charles H. Memorial Funeral Chapel College Station website, January 12, 2012. www.dignitymemorial.com

Buckley, John Laguinn. Find a Grave website, June 17, 1997. www.findagrave.com

Gaskamp, Robert E. *Houston Chronicle* website, February 23, 2002. www.houstonchronicle.com

Giddings, Dr. Thomas. *Houston Chronicle* website, November 6, 2000. www
.houstonchronicle.com

Hasskarl, W. F. "Boy," Jr. Brenham Memorial Chapel Funeral Home website,
August 9, 2008. www.brenhammemorialchapel.com

Kruse, Ken Eddie. *Brenham Banner-Press,* April 1, 1999.

Kruse, Neil Howard. *Brenham Banner-Press,* August 11, 2003.

Schomburg, Dennis William Jr. Brenham Memorial Chapel Funeral Home
website, October 1, 2005. www.brenhammemorialchapel.com

Seelhorst, Ernest Henry. Brenham Memorial Chapel Funeral Home website,
April 4, 2008. www.brenhammemorialchapel.com

Strickel, Johnson D. "Shady." Texas A&M University Foundation website,
March 7, 2007. www.tamugift.org

Tiaden, Hildegard Sophie Steinbach. Ancestry website, April 1, 2007. www
.ancestry.com

Trostle, Maurice Eugene "Shorty." Brenham Memorial Chapel Funeral
Home website, December 26, 2008. www.brenhammemorialchapel.com

Wiese, Omer Beatrice Slagle. Find a Grave website, November 1, 2003. www
.findagrave.com

Winkelmann, Frederick Christian Jr. Brenham Memorial Chapel Funeral
Home website, October 30, 2006. www.brenhammemorialchapel.com

FAMILY TREASURES

"About Us." Quebe Guesthouse, n.d. www.quebefarm.com

Klausmeyer, Evelyn Sander. *Descendants of August Friedrich Wilhelm and Wilhelmine Lippe Kruse,* 2006.

Kruse, Ed. F. "A Dad's Comments on His Son, Neil, for the Benefit of Jordan, Claire, and Their Offspring." December 2, 2008.

———. "To Our Children's Children." 1994.

Kruse, Evelyn D. "Recipe—Evelyn's Bread Pudding." December 4, 1996.

Kruse, Janie. "Our Story." 2008.

"Memorial Service for Dr. Neil Howard Kruse." August 18, 2003.

"Prairie Hill Cemetery." St. John Lutheran Church of Prairie Hill, n.d. www
.stjohnprairiehill.org

MISCELLANEOUS

Dairy Training and Merchandizing Institute (affiliate of the International Association of Ice Cream Manufacturers and the Milk Industry

Foundation). Certificate to Ed. F. Kruse for completing a two-week "Management Development Program for Dairy Executives," March 11, 1967.

"Edward F. Kruse '49—Distinguished Alumnus of Texas A&M University 2005." [See article and video on page 13 under "Name"]. www.aggienetwork.com/tribute/.

"Football Contest: Brenham Cubs, Champions of District 33A vs. El Campo Rice Birds, Champions of District 34A. Cub Stadium, Friday, December 8, 1945. 8:00 PM." Football program, December 8, 1945.

Goeke, Ruth. Answers to All Questions Asked with Reference to this Project from May 2012–February 2015.

———. Biographical Information—E. F. Kruse, n.d.

———. Ed. F. Kruse—Biographical and Philanthropic Information. 2014.

———. List of Ed's Sayings (aka "Edisms"). May 23, 2012.

———. "Mr. E. F. Kruse." n.d.

———. "Philanthropy in the 1990s." A summary of Ed and Evelyn Kruse's contributions, 1990–1999.

———. "Recognition of Ed Kruse for Serving 50 Years on the Board." December 11, 2001.

Handwritten "bets" between Ed and Howard Kruse concerning future events in the ice cream market. June 21, 1978.

Hope, Bob. A list of jokes sent to Ed. F. Kruse from a friend via email, December 10, 2007.

Kruse, Ed. F. "Beauty Pageant Questions." June 4, 2002.

———. Introduction to a talk at a Dairy Products Institute meeting, n.d.

———. Notes for a talk for a Blue Bell Ice Cream class, Brenham, Texas, 1999.

———. Outline for a talk for a Blue Bell Ice Cream class. Circa 1990.

———. Outline for a talk for a Blue Bell sales training seminar, n.d.

———. Outline for talk upon receiving the Kupfer Award at the Mays Business School at Texas A&M University. College Station, Texas, October 21, 2005.

———. "Red Letter Dates at Blue Bell." 1994.

———. "Things to Remember (aka 'Edisms')." Outline for a speech to a Blue Bell Ice Cream class, November 14, 2009.

———. "Travelogue: Trip to Australia–New Zealand." February 11, 1989–March 11, 1989.

———. "Travelogue: Trip to South Africa." May 1998.

"Resolution." Blue Bell Creameries recognizing Ed. F. Kruse upon his retirement as chairman of the board, February 26, 2014.

"Resolution." Texas H. R. No. 688 recognizing Faburn Moses Murray on his 79th birthday, March 2, 2007.

"Rotary Wheel." Directory of members of Brenham Rotary, August 3, 1954.

Texas Lutheran University. "The Edward F. and Evelyn D. Kruse Scholarship for Education and Pre-Theology: Biographical Information." Information given to the public upon the creation of this scholarship. 2009.

"The Barbara Bush Rose Garden and Pavilion." Program for the ribbon-cutting ceremony at the George Bush Presidential Library and Museum. College Station, Texas, April 10, 2006.

[Index]